Bond

Maths
Assessment Papers

10–11+ years
Book 2

David Clemson

UNIVERSITY PRESS

UNIVERSITY PRESS

Great Clarendon Street, Oxford, OX2 6DP, United Kingdom

Oxford University Press is a department of the University of Oxford. It furthers the University's objective of excellence in research, scholarship, and education by publishing worldwide. Oxford is a registered trade mark of Oxford University Press in the UK and in certain other countries

First published in 2007 by Nelson Thornes Ltd
This edition published in 2014

British Library Cataloguing in Publication Data
Data available

978-1-4085-2528-9

10 9 8 7 6 5 4 3 2 1

Printed in China

Acknowledgements

Page make-up: OKS Prepress, India
Illustrations: Tech-Set Limited

Before you get started

What is Bond?

This book is part of the Bond Assessment Papers series for maths, which provides **thorough and continuous practice of all the key maths content** from ages five to thirteen. Bond's maths resources are ideal preparation for many different kinds of tests and exams – from SATs to 11+ and other secondary school selection exams.

How does the scope of this book match real exam content?

Maths 10–11+ Book 1 and *Book 2* are the core Bond 11+ books. Each paper is **pitched at the level of a typical 11+ exam** and covers the key maths a child would be expected to learn. The papers are also in line with other selective exams for this age group. The coverage is matched to the National Curriculum and the National Numeracy Strategy and will also **provide invaluable preparation for Key Stage 2 SATs**. One of the key features of Bond Assessment Papers is that each one practises **a wide variety of skills and question types** so that children are always challenged to think – and don't get bored repeating the same question type again and again. We think that variety is the key to effective learning. It helps children 'think on their feet' and cope with the unexpected.

What does the book contain?

- **23 papers** – each one contains 50 questions.
- **Tutorial links throughout** – B 5 – this icon appears in the margin next to the questions. It indicates links to the relevant section in *How to do … 11+ Maths*, our invaluable subject guide that offers explanations and practice for all core question types.
- **Scoring devices** – there are score boxes in the margins and a progress chart on page 76. The chart is a visual and motivating way for children to see how they are doing. It also turns the score into a percentage that can help decide what to do next.
- **Next Steps Planner** – advice on what to do after finishing the papers can be found on the inside back cover.
- **Answers** – located in an easily-removed central pull-out section.

How can you use this book?

One of the great strengths of Bond Assessment Papers is their flexibility. They can be used at home, in school and by tutors to:

- set **timed formal practice** tests – allow about 30 minutes per paper in line with standard 11+ demands. Reduce the suggested time limit by five minutes to practise working at speed.

- provide **bite-sized chunks** for regular practice.
- **highlight strengths and weaknesses** in the core skills.
- identify **individual needs**.
- set **homework**.
- follow **a complete 11+ preparation strategy** alongside *The Parents' Guide to the 11+* (see below).

It is best to start at the beginning and work through the papers in order. Calculators should not be used.

Remind children to check whether each answer needs a unit of measurement before they start a test. If units of measurement are not included in answers that require them, they will lose marks for those questions. To ensure that children can practise including them in their answers, units of measurement have been omitted after the answer rules for some questions.

If you are using the book as part of a careful run-in to the 11+, we suggest that you also have two other essential Bond resources close at hand:

How to do … 11+ Maths: the subject guide that explains all the question types practised in this book. Use the cross-reference icons to find the relevant sections.

The Parents' Guide to the 11+: the step-by-step guide to the whole 11+ experience. It clearly explains the 11+ process, provides guidance on how to assess children, helps you to set complete action plans for practice and explains how you can use the *Maths 10-11⁺ Book 1* and *Book 2* as part of a strategic run-in to the exam.

See the inside front cover for more details of these books.

What does a score mean and how can it be improved?

It is unfortunately impossible to guarantee that a child will pass the 11+ exam if they achieve a certain score on any practice book or paper. Success on the day depends on a host of factors, including the scores of the other children sitting the test. However, we can give some guidance on what a score indicates and how to improve it.

If children colour in the progress chart on page 76, this will give an idea of present performance in percentage terms. The Next Steps Planner inside the back cover will help you to decide what to do next to help a child progress. It is always valuable to go over wrong answers with children. If they are having trouble with any particular question type, follow the tutorial links to *How to do … 11+ Maths* for step-by-step explanations and further practice.

Don't forget the website …!

Visit www.bond11plus.co.uk for lots of advice, information and suggestions on everything to do with Bond, the 11+ and helping children to do their best.

Key words

Some special maths words are used in this book. You will find them **in bold** each time they appear in the papers. These words are explained here.

acute angle an angle that is less than a right angle

coordinates the two numbers, the first horizontal the second vertical, that plot a point on a grid, for example (3, 2)

factor the factors of a number are numbers that divide into it, for example 1, 2, 4 and 8 are all factors of 8

kite a four-sided shape that looks like a stretched diamond

lowest term the simplest you can make a fraction, for example $\frac{4}{10}$ reduced to the lowest term is $\frac{2}{5}$

mean one kind of average. You find the mean by adding all the scores together and dividing by the number of scores, for example the mean of 1, 3 and 8 is 4

median one kind of average. The middle number of a set of numbers after being ordered from lowest to highest, for example the median of 1, 3 and 8 is 3

mixed number a number that contains a whole number and a fraction, for example $5\frac{1}{2}$ is a mixed number

mode one kind of average. The most common number in a set of numbers, for example the mode of 2, 3, 2, 7, 2 is 2

obtuse angle an angle that is more than 90° and not more than 180°

parallelogram a four-sided shape that has all its opposite sides equal and parallel

polygon a closed shape with three or more sides

prime factor the factors of a number that are also prime numbers, for example the prime factors of 12 are 2 and 3

prime number any number that can only be divided by itself or 1. 2, 3 and 7 are prime numbers. (Note that 1 is not a prime number.)

quotient the answer if you divide one number by another, for example the quotient of 12 ÷ 4 is 3

range the difference between the largest and smallest of a set of numbers, for example the range of 1, 2, 5, 3, 6, 8 is 7

reflex angle an angle that is bigger than 180° and less than 360°

rhombus a four-sided shape, like a squashed square, that has all its sides of equal length and its opposite sides parallel

trapezium a four-sided shape that has just one pair of parallel sides

vertex, vertices the point where two or more edges or sides in a shape meet

Paper 1

Write these in figures.

1 two hundred thousand and twenty   _____

2 forty-nine thousand and forty-nine   _____

A map uses a scale of 1:100 000.

3 If a road is 5 km long, how long will it be on the map?   _____ cm

Put the appropriate signs in these calculations to make them correct.

4 102 ___ 6 = 17   **5** 48 ___ 4 = 12   **6** 4 ___ (9 × 8) = 76

7 (8 × 12) ___ 5 = 91   **8** 12 + (8 ___ 3) = 17   **9–10** (11 ___ 6) ___ 9 = 45

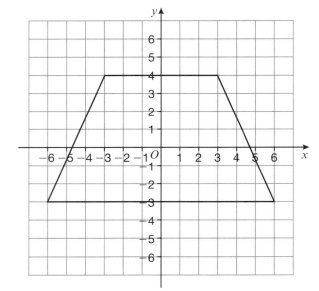

Write the **coordinates** of this shape.

11–14 (___ , ___) (___ , ___) (___ , ___) (___ , ___)

15 What is the name of the shape above?   _____

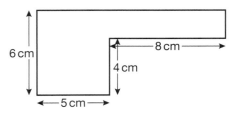

16 What is the perimeter of the shape?   _____ cm

17 What is the area of the shape?   _____ cm²

B | 1

B26/B3

3

B3/B2

7

B | 23

B | 19

5

B | 20

2

Circle the smallest in each of these groups.

18 $\frac{1}{3}$ of 8 $\frac{2}{3}$ of 12 $\frac{1}{2}$ of 14 $\frac{3}{4}$ of 16 $\frac{3}{5}$ of 15

19 $\frac{5}{8}$ $\frac{1}{2}$ $\frac{1}{6}$ $\frac{2}{8}$ $\frac{3}{8}$

20 $\frac{17}{40}$ $\frac{40}{40}$ $\frac{8}{10}$ $\frac{4}{5}$ $\frac{35}{50}$

21   0.33 $\frac{2}{3}$ $\frac{5}{6}$ 0.4 $\frac{1}{4}$

22   507   0.507   50.7   0.0507   5.07

A local football club did a survey of 96 of their spectators.

They drew this pie chart showing the age ranges of these fans.

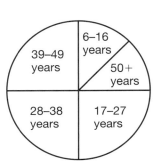

23 What fraction is in the age range 28–38? _____

24 What fraction is in the age range 6–16? _____

25 What percentage is in the age range 39–49? _____

26 How many spectators are over 16? _____

27 How many 6–27-year-olds are there? _____

28 How many spectators are not aged between 17 and 49? _____

Write the **mode**, **median** and **mean** of these sets of numbers.

29–31 10   5   6   8   6

The mode is _____   The median is _____   The mean is _____

32–34 12   15   19   18   15   22   25

The mode is _____   The median is _____   The mean is _____

35–38 Write down the numbers that will come out of this machine.

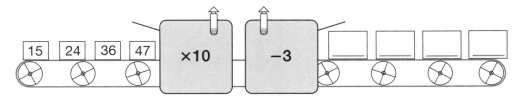

39 Kamal buys his lunches Monday to Friday and they cost £p per day. He buys lunch on the weekends for £q per day. Expressed as an equation, how much does Kamal spend each week on lunch? _____

40 Multiply 10.06 by 10. _____

3

Divide these by 100 to give a **quotient**.

41 265 _____

42 138.8 _____

43 406.15 _____

3

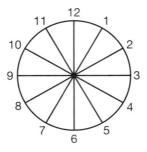

What is the size of the smaller angle between:

44 2 and 4? _____°

45 4 and 9? _____°

46 9 and 10? _____°

47 8 and 12? _____°

4

Between them Anish, Jason and Rob have 40 swap cards. Jason has twice as many as Anish, and Rob has five times as many as Anish.

48 How many does Anish have? _____

49 How many does Jason have? _____

50 How many does Rob have? _____

3

Now go to the Progress Chart to record your score! **Total** 50

Paper 2

1–4 Solve these calculations.

$$\begin{array}{r} 458 \\ 394 \\ + 825 \\ \hline \end{array}$$
$$\begin{array}{r} 423 \\ \times 8 \\ \hline \end{array}$$
$$13\overline{)2873}$$
$$\begin{array}{r} 337 \\ \times 45 \\ \hline \end{array}$$

4

Multiply these by 100.

5 56.15 _____

6 13.06 _____

7 0.107 _____

3

Divide these by 100.

8 3126 _____

9 458.5 _____

10 11.73 _____

3

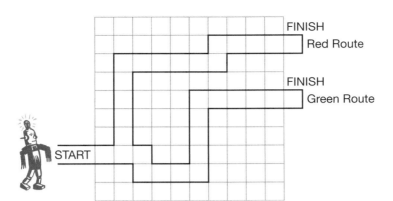

11–12 The robot is on START. Guide it along the two routes shown above to reach the FINISH. It can only move Forward, Turn Right 90° and Turn Left 90°. Circle one letter (A, B, C, D, E, or F) and write RED on the relevant answer line to indicate the correct instructions for the Red route. Circle a different letter and write GREEN to indicate the Green route.

A Forward 3, Turn Right 90°, Forward 4, Turn Left 90°, Forward 6,
Turn Right 90°, Forward 4, Turn Left 90°, Forward 2. _____

B Forward 2, Turn Left 90°, Forward 5, Turn Right 90°, Forward 4,
Turn Left 90°, Forward 4, Turn Left 90°, Forward 2. _____

C Forward 2, Turn Left 90°, Forward 5, Turn Right 90°, Forward 5,
Turn Left 90°, Forward 1, Turn Right 90°, Forward 4. _____

D Forward 3, Turn Right 90°, Forward 3, Turn Left 90°, Forward 4,
Turn Left 90°, Forward 5, Turn Right 90°, Forward 6. _____

E Forward 3, Turn Right 90°, Forward 1, Turn Left 90°, Forward 3,
Turn Left 90°, Forward 4, Turn Right 90°, Forward 5. _____

F Forward 3, Turn Right 90°, Forward 1, Turn Right 90°, Forward 3,
Turn Left 90°, Forward 4, Turn Right 90°, Forward 5. _____

2

When I roll a fair dice what is the probability (expressed in **lowest term** fraction) that I will get:

13 an odd number? _____   **14** a six? _____   **15** a 2 or a 4? _____

3

16 Calculate the area of a square with a perimeter of 20 cm.   _____ cm²

1

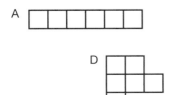
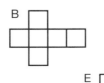
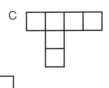

17–18 Circle the letters to indicate which of these nets would fold to make a closed cube.

2

5

A `22:17`   B `13:05`   C `14:22`

19–21 What times will these digital clocks show in $3\frac{1}{4}$ hours time?

A __ : __   B __ : __   C __ : __

A `16:10`   B `17:27`   C `02:00`

22–24 What times did these digital clocks show $2\frac{3}{4}$ hours ago?

A __ : __   B __ : __   C __ : __

25–28 Write these fractions as decimals.

$7\frac{1}{2}$ $9\frac{1}{20}$ $6\frac{4}{40}$ $8\frac{9}{50}$

_____   _____   _____   _____

Put the appropriate signs in these calculations to make them correct.

29 63 ___ 6 = 10.5   **30** 63 ___ 6 = 69   **31** 63 ___ 6 = 57

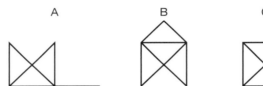

A   B   C   D

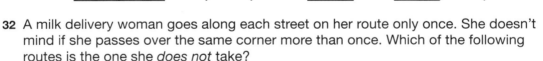

32 A milk delivery woman goes along each street on her route only once. She doesn't mind if she passes over the same corner more than once. Which of the following routes is the one she *does not* take?

Rashid has three kinds of music on his MP3 player: Classical, Rock and Pop. He has four times as many Pop as Classical, and three times as many Rock as Classical. Altogether Rashid has 80 tracks.

33 How many Classical tracks does he have?   _____

34 How many Rock tracks does he have?   _____

35 How many Pop tracks does he have?   _____

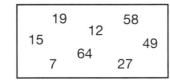

```
      19        58
          12
  15            49
       64
    7        27
```

36–39 Put circles around the **prime numbers** and squares around the square numbers.

 B 27
 B 10
 6
 B 10
 B 11
 4
 B3/B2
 3
 1
 B 4
 B 13
 3
 B 6
 4

What is the **median** in each of these sets of numbers?

40 15   17   21   14   19   22   16   _____

41 27   103   48   59   101   77   85   _____

What is the **mode** in each of these sets of numbers?

42 36   40   41   36   35   40   36   _____

43 0.8   0.75   0.5   0.4   0.5   0.1   0.8   0.5   _____

What is the **mean** in each of these sets of numbers?

44 1.5   2.5   7.5   5.0   3.5   _____

45 110   106   112   120   124   118   _____

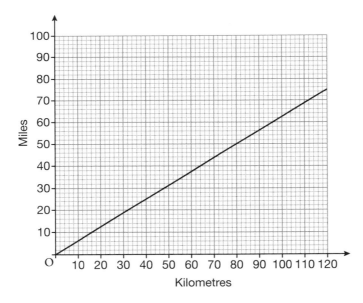

Use this line graph, which is a conversion graph from miles to kilometres and from kilometres to miles, to answer these questions.

46 What is 50 miles in kilometres?   _____ km

47 What is 120 kilometres in miles?   _____ miles

48 Approximately how many miles is 70 kilometres?   _____ miles

49 Approximately how many kilometres is 60 miles?   _____ km

50 Which is the greater, 25 miles or 35 kilometres?   _____

Paper 3

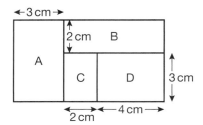

I made this large rectangle from four smaller ones.

1 What is the area of rectangle A? _____

2 What is the area of rectangle B? _____

3 What is the area of rectangle C? _____

4 What is the area of rectangle D? _____

5 What is the perimeter of the large rectangle? _____

6–11 A local computer shop is putting up its prices. Everything will go up by $12\frac{1}{2}\%$. Complete this table.

Price	Price rise	Total price
£20	£_____	£_____
£50	£_____	£_____
£100	£_____	£_____

12 Orla's angelfish had a **mean** number of 9 babies each. There are 72 baby angelfish in her tank. How many mother angelfish does she have? _____

What number does each symbol represent?

13 ▲ × 7 = (2 × 6) + (2 × 8)   ▲ = _____

14 12 + 15 = 3 × ●   ● = _____

15 4 × 11 = (2 × 2) + (8 × ■)   ■ = _____

Jerzy put 54 strawberries into small, medium and large bowls in the ratio 1 : 2 : 3. How many are in:

16 the small bowl? _____

17 the medium bowl? _____

18 the large bowl? _____

19–20 What is 4^2? _____

What **prime number** is closest to this? _____

B 6
2

21–22 What is 6^2? _____

What **prime number** is closest to this? _____

B 6
2

Calculate the area of these triangles.
Scale: each square represents 1 cm^2.

B 18

23 _____ 24 _____ 25 _____ 26 _____

4

Write these to the nearest 10.

27 583 _____ 28 737 _____

B 1
2

Write these to the nearest 100.

29 1549 _____ 30 2378 _____

B 1
2

Write these to the nearest 1000.

31 23 501 _____ 32 79 605 _____

B 1
2

B 27

18 minutes

Craggytown
(10 minutes at the quay)

Bluestrands
Bay

Sandyville
(10 minutes at the quay)

14 minutes

33–37 A ferry crosses Bluestrands Bay from Craggytown to Sandyville and back again all day. Here is a part of the ferry timetable for one morning when the tide makes the journey from Sandyville to Craggytown quicker than the other way. Fill in the missing sailing times.

Leave Craggytown	Leave Sandyville
9:00 a.m.	_____ a.m.
_____ a.m.	_____ a.m.
_____ a.m.	_____ a.m.

5

Give the answer to each calculation using the combined forms of measurement shown.

38 589 cm + 392 cm = _____ m _____ cm

39 607 cm − 209 cm = _____ m _____ cm

40 770 cm × 5 = _____ m _____ cm

41 1506 g + 2344 g = _____ kg _____ g

42 4380 g − 1820 g = _____ kg _____ g

Here are some prices in a local shop.

Bottle of fabric softener	£1.69
Pack of scouring pads	£1.99
Packet of soap powder	£2.49
Bottle of washing-up liquid	£1.58

43–44 Wasim bought two of these items and got 52p change from a £5.00 note. Which two did Wasim buy? _____ and _____

45 What would be the cost of five packs of scouring pads? £ _____

46 Melanie bought a bottle of fabric softener, a pack of scouring pads and a bottle of washing-up liquid. What change was she given from a £20 note? £ _____

47–50 In a nearby shop there was a sale in which everything was being sold at a third off. Complete this table to show the original, full price.

Sale price	Original, full price
£6.46	_____
£10.86	_____
£12.50	_____
£58.24	_____

Now go to the Progress Chart to record your score! **Total** 50

Paper 4

You spin this hexagonal spinner with coloured segments. Circle the correct probability for these spins.

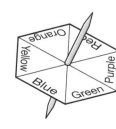

1 What is the probability of spinning red?

$\frac{1}{3}$ $\frac{2}{3}$ $\frac{1}{2}$ $\frac{1}{6}$

2 What is the probability of spinning green?

$\frac{1}{2}$ $\frac{1}{5}$ $\frac{1}{6}$ $\frac{2}{5}$

B 25
B 2
B 3
5

B 2
B 3
B 4
4

B 10
4

B 16

3 What is the probability of spinning purple, orange or yellow?

$\frac{1}{6}$ $\qquad$ $\frac{1}{2}$ $\qquad$ $\frac{5}{6}$ $\qquad$ $\frac{2}{3}$

4 What is the probability of spinning blue or purple?

$\frac{2}{3}$ $\qquad$ $\frac{1}{3}$ $\qquad$ $\frac{5}{6}$ $\qquad$ $\frac{2}{5}$

Which numbers are the arrows pointing to on this number line?

5 Arrow A _____

6 Arrow B _____

7 Arrow C _____

8 Arrow D _____

What number does each letter represent?

9 $4 \times a = 14 - 2$ $\qquad\qquad\qquad$ $a = $ _____

10 $(5 \times b) - (2 \times b) = 15$ $\qquad\qquad$ $b = $ _____

11 $(3 \times c) + c = 12$ $\qquad\qquad\qquad$ $c = $ _____

12 $(4 \times d) + (3 \times d) = 28$ $\qquad\quad$ $d = $ _____

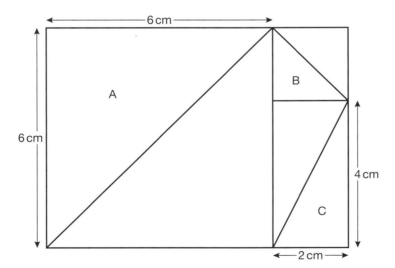

I made this large rectangle from six triangles.
Write in the area of:

13 triangle A _____ $\qquad$ **14** triangle B _____

15 triangle C _____ $\qquad$ **16** the large rectangle _____

17–19 Some digits are missing in these calculations. Write them in.

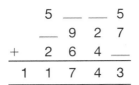

$$
\begin{array}{r}
5\ \_\_\ \_\_\ 5 \\
\_\_\ 9\ 2\ 7 \\
+\ \ 2\ 6\ 4\ \_\_ \\
\hline
1\ 1\ 7\ 4\ 3
\end{array}
$$

$$
\begin{array}{r}
1\ \_\_\ 8\ \_\_ \\
-\ \ 8\ \_\_\ 9 \\
\hline
8\ 2\ 4
\end{array}
$$

$$
\begin{array}{r}
4\ 5\ 6 \\
\times\ \ \ \ \ \ \ \_\_ \\
\hline
2\ 2\ 8\ 0
\end{array}
$$

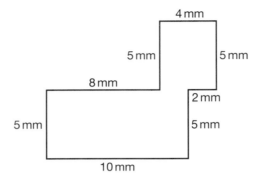

4 mm

5 mm   5 mm

8 mm

2 mm

5 mm   5 mm

10 mm

20 What is the perimeter of this shape? _____

21 What is the area of this shape? _____

2

Divide each of these by 100.

22 1.65 _____   **23** 0.483 _____

24 0.3217 _____   **25** 0.0791 _____

4

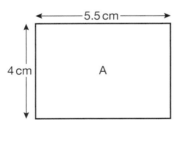

5.5 cm

4 cm   A

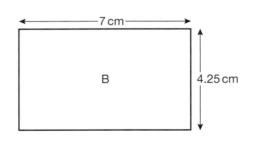

7 cm

B   4.25 cm

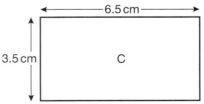

6.5 cm

3.5 cm   C

Calculate the area and the perimeter of each of these rectangles.

26–27 A: Area = _____ cm²   Perimeter = _____ cm

28–29 B: Area = _____ cm²   Perimeter = _____ cm

30–31 C: Area = _____ cm²   Perimeter = _____ cm

6

Here are some mathematics test results.

15   26   30   40   26   17   43   34   28   44   38   19

B 15

32 What is the **range**? _____

33 What is the **median**? _____

34 What is the **mode**? _____

35 What is the **mean**? _____

Underline the correct answer to each of these calculations.

B 11
B 3

36 $0.25 \times 0.25 =$ 62.5   6.25   0.625   0.0625   0.006 25

37 $736 \div 200 =$ 8.36   3.68   3.86   6.83   6.38

38 $0.316 \div 0.4 =$ 0.0079   0.079   79   0.79   7.9

Complete these calculations.

B 3

39   _____
36)1332

40   _____
24)1152

41   _____
39)1053

Divide these numbers by 10.

B 1

42 21.73   _____

43 5.46   _____

44 0.189   _____

A `15:26`   B `08:30`   C `2 1: 18`

B 27
B 10

45–50 What will the time be in $1\frac{3}{4}$ hours? Write the answer first for a 24-hour clock, then for a 12-hour clock.

A __ : __   or _____

B __ : __   or _____

C __ : __   or _____

Now go to the Progress Chart to record your score!   Total ◯ 50

Paper 5

In a survey, 300 families were asked where in Europe they went on holiday last year. Here are their replies in percentages.

B 12
B 2

Austria	6%	Belgium	4%
France	23%	Germany	3%
Greece	10%	Ireland	4%
Italy	6%	Netherlands	3%
Spain	35%	Switzerland	4%
Other countries	2%		

1 How many people went to France? _____

2 Which was the most popular destination? _____

3 How many families went to Austria or Switzerland? _____

4 How many families went to Germany or Belgium? _____

5 How many fewer families went to Greece than to Spain? _____

I went shopping yesterday. It took me 15 minutes to walk to the first shop where I stayed for 38 minutes. Three minutes later I entered another shop and stayed there for 27 minutes. Then I walked home taking 21 minutes to do so. I left home at 9:30 a.m.

B 27

6 What time did I get back home? _____ a.m.

7 What time did I enter the second shop? _____ a.m.

Complete these sequences.

B 7

8–9	256	128	64	32	_____	_____
10–11	53	49	45	41	_____	_____
12–13	7	14	28	56	_____	_____

14–18 A bike shop increased its prices by 10%. Complete the table.

B 12

Old price	New price
£60	£ _____
£200	£ _____
£340	£ _____
£255	£ _____
£405	£ _____

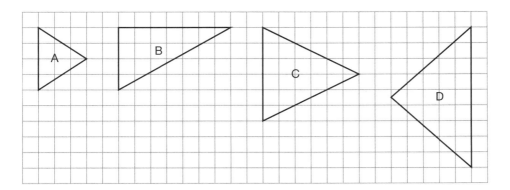

Find the area of these triangles.
Scale: each square represents 1 cm^2.

19–22 A _____   B _____   C _____   D _____

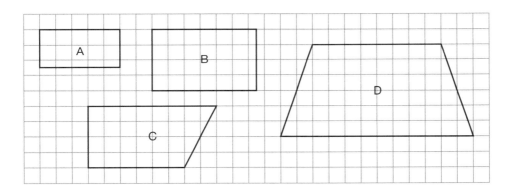

Now find the area of these shapes.
Scale: each square represents 1 cm^2.

23–26 A _____   B _____   C _____   D _____

British pounds	US dollars	Euros	Indian rupees	Philippine pesos
£1	1.87	1.46	87	96

27 How many euros do you get for £50?   € _____

28 How many Indian rupees do you get for £50?   _____ rupees

29 How many British pounds do you get for 374 US dollars?   £ _____

30 How many Philippine pesos do you get for £200?   _____ pesos

31 An article costs £6.75. How much would 6 of these articles cost?   £ _____

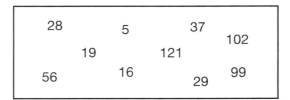

Circle TRUE or FALSE for each of these statements.

32 Line C is parallel to Line H.   TRUE   FALSE

33 Line G is vertical.   TRUE   FALSE

34 Line B is horizontal.   TRUE   FALSE

35 Line D is parallel to Line H.   TRUE   FALSE

36 Line E is perpendicular to Line H.   TRUE   FALSE

37 Line A is perpendicular to Line F.   TRUE   FALSE

38–41 Draw a circle around the **prime numbers** in this box.

28	5	37	
19	121		102
56	16	29	99

Turn the following lengths into kilometres.

42 1897 m = _____ km

43 23 873 m = _____ km

44 632 m = _____ km

45 Annushka rides her horse at a steady canter and covers 5 metres every second. If it takes them 80 seconds to canter around the edge of the home paddock, what is the perimeter of the paddock? _____ m

46 The **mean** of the following ten numbers is 2.4. Find the missing number.

2   6   1   2   3   2   1   4   1   _____

B 17

6

B 6

4

B 25

B4/B3

B 20

4

B 15

1

A swimming pool contains 4 million litres of water.

B 1
B 10

47 When it is $\frac{1}{5}$ full how many litres are in it? _____ litres

B 12

48 What % of the content is 600 000 litres? _____%

B 3

49 For cleaning it is filled with only $\frac{1}{50}$ of its entire contents.
How much water is this? _____ litres

50 If the pool has eight lanes, how much water is in each lane? _____ litres

4

Now go to the Progress Chart to record your score!   **Total**   50

Paper 6

Here are some of the highest mountains in the UK. Write the height of each to the nearest 100 feet.

B 1

1 Ben Nevis, Scotland	4408 feet	_____ feet
2 Ben Macdhui, Scotland	4296 feet	_____ feet
3 Ben Lawers, Scotland	3984 feet	_____ feet
4 Snowdon, Wales	3560 feet	_____ feet
5 Scafell Pike, England	3206 feet	_____ feet
6 Slieve Donard, N. Ireland	2796 feet	_____ feet

6

Put the correct sign $<$, $>$ or $=$ in these calculations.

A 6
B 3

7 7×8 ____ 5×11

B 2

8 $11 + 9 + 10$ ____ $29 + 2$

B6/B3

9 6^2 ____ 4×9

B 25

10 $0.75\,m$ ____ $760\,cm$

B27/10

11 $105\,min$ ____ $1\frac{3}{4}$ hour

B3/B6

12 5×10 ____ 7^2

6

13–15 Write down the numbers that will come out of this machine.

B 9

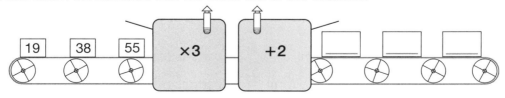

| 19 | 38 | 55 | ×3 | +2 |

3

17

A bag contains 5 grey balls, 4 white balls and 1 black ball. Underline the correct answer to each question.

B 16

16 What is the probability of picking a grey ball?

$\frac{4}{5}$ $\frac{1}{2}$ $\frac{3}{5}$ $\frac{1}{5}$ $\frac{1}{10}$

17 What is the probability of picking a black ball?

$\frac{1}{100}$ $\frac{1}{10}$ $\frac{1}{5}$ $\frac{4}{5}$

18 What is the probability of picking a white ball?

$\frac{1}{5}$ $\frac{2}{5}$ $\frac{3}{5}$ $\frac{4}{5}$ $\frac{9}{10}$

19 What is the probability of picking a ball that is not grey, white or black?

$\frac{1}{10}$ $\frac{3}{5}$ 0 $\frac{1}{2}$

4

B 17
B 18

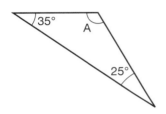 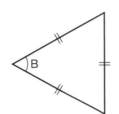  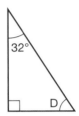

20–23 Calculate these angles.

A = _____ °   B = _____ °   C = _____ °   D = _____ °

4

B 3
B 25

24–27 In the chiller cabinet in my local shop there are supplies of fresh cream and milk. If the following supplies were in the cabinet on two different days, how much cream and milk was there?

Day 1:   6 pots of cream = _____ ml   8 cartons of milk = __ l _____ ml

Day 2: 14 pots of cream = __ l _____ ml   11 cartons of milk = __ l _____ ml

4

Solve these calculations.

B2/B3

28   6839
   + 2165

   _____

29 (9 × 8) + 25 =   _____

30 (275 ÷ 22) + 7 =   _____

31
   $\overline{}$
   16$\overline{)304}$

32
   $\overline{}$
   28$\overline{)896}$

33 9.3 − 5.4 =   _____   6

Insert the missing signs to make these statements correct.   B2/B3

34–35 (6 ___ 4) ___ 5 = 2

36–37 6 ___ 3 ___ 2 = 9

38–39 5 ___ 4 ___ 2 = 7   6

Turn the following lengths into metres.   B 25

40 365 cm = _____   **41** 15 678 cm = _____   2

B 20

$$2x$$

$$x$$

42 What is the area of this shape?   _____   1

43–45 What are the **prime factors** of 42?   _____ , _____ and _____   B5/B6

3

Calculate these percentages.   B 12

46 15% of 240 =   _____

47 25% of 112 =   _____

48 30% of 1860 =   _____

49 75% of 96 =   _____

50 15% of 300 =   _____   5

Paper 7

1 Last year, in months with 31 days, I collected *m* tokens.
In months with 30 days I collected *2m* tokens.
For the rest of the year I collected *3m* tokens.
How many tokens did I collect last year? _____

Round these numbers to the nearest 1000.

2 63 501 _____

3 128 609 _____

British pounds	Euros	NZ dollars	Thailand baht
1	1.5	3	70

How much would these items be in British pounds?

4 A pair of trainers costing 42 euros. £ _____

5 A packet of biscuits costing 6 NZ dollars. £ _____

6 A cake costing 245 baht. £ _____

Write these **mixed numbers** in their **lowest terms**.

7 $4\frac{12}{18}$ _____

8 $6\frac{25}{75}$ _____

9 $3\frac{14}{21}$ _____

Write these decimals as fractions in their **lowest terms**.

10 2.6 _____

11 10.4 _____

12 3.05 _____

13 7.75 _____

Find the answers to these calculations.

14 $6.5 + 3.05 =$ _____

15 $4 \times 1.25 =$ _____

16 $3.75 - 2.95 =$ _____

17 $9 \div 0.3 =$ _____

18 Three roadside flashing beacons are all switched on at the same time. One flashes every 6 seconds, one every 9 seconds and the third every 12 seconds. How many seconds after being switched on do they flash at the same time?

_____ seconds

B4/B5

1

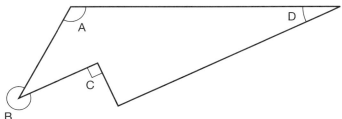

B 4

19–22 Use **acute**, **obtuse**, right-angled or **reflex** to describe the angles marked A–D.

A _____   B _____   C _____   D _____

4

Jack is a window cleaner. He carries three ladders. The shortest ladder is half as long as the middle ladder. The longest ladder is twice as long as the middle ladder. If he joins all of the ladders together he can climb 42 feet.

B 4
B 13

23–25 How long is each ladder?

Shortest _____ feet

Middle _____ feet

Longest _____ feet

3

Fifteen children sat a science test. Here are their results:

B 15

30	32	28	29	30	28	30	26
27	28	26	27	26	30	30	

26 What is the **mode**? _____

27 What is the **range**? _____

28 What is the **median**? _____

3

29 The total marks obtained in a mathematics test were 384. If the **mean** was 24, how many children took the test? _____

B 15
1

Find the answers to these calculations.

B 25

30 $6.3\,m + 12.8\,m + 73.5\,m =$ _____ m

B 2

31 $160\,ml + 820\,ml + 0.5\,l =$ _____ l

32 $803\,g + 1.6\,kg + 326\,g =$ _____ kg

3

This is the plan of a formal garden.
All of the paths are 2 m wide.
The rose beds are square, and the shrub beds are rectangles of equal size.

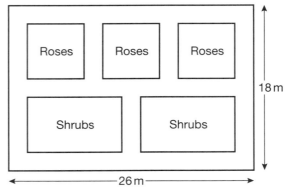

B 20

33 What is the area of a rose bed? _____

34 What is the area of a shrub bed? _____

35 What is the perimeter of a rose bed? _____

36 What is the perimeter of a shrub bed? _____

4

B 6

37 What is 9^2? _____

38 What is 49 written as a square number? _____

2

B 23

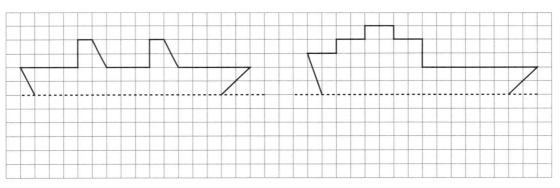

39–40 Draw in the reflections of these two ships.

2

41–44 Karla manages four salespeople. She decides to give each of them a 7.5% rise in salary. What are their new salaries?

B 12

Name	Salary	New salary
Mrs Jones	£21 000	£ _____
Mr Yusef	£18 000	£ _____
Ms Samson	£19 000	£ _____
Mr Smith	£20 500	£ _____

4

TV1 and TV2 are television channels both showing films that start at 8:30 p.m.
TV1 puts on advertisements every 10 minutes after the start of a film.
TV2 puts on advertisements every 15 minutes after the start of a film.

45 What is the earliest time that there will be advertisements on both
channels at the same time? _____ p.m.

46 If the shortest film ends after 2 hours, how many times (during the films) will
advertisements appear on both channels at the same time? _____

2

Here is a list of some of the largest lakes in the world. Write the area of each lake to the
nearest 1000 km².

B 1

47 Lake Victoria   62 940 km² _____

48 Lake Huron   59 580 km² _____

49 Lake Michigan   57 700 km² _____

50 Lake Baikal   31 494 km² _____

4

Now go to the Progress Chart to record your score!   **Total**   50

Paper 8

B3/B4

B 2

1 One cross-stitch picture needs 529 cross stitches to make it. How many
cross stitches are there in 13 pictures? _____

2 A garden wall needs 35 rows of 228 bricks. How many bricks is this? _____

3 The library van delivers 1014 books to a school for 13 groups of children.
How many books are there for each group? _____

4 There are 11 players in a football team. There are enough children in a
school to make 17 football teams with 2 substitutes for each team.
How many children are there in the school? _____

4

5 Which of the following shapes has a perimeter of 10 cm? Circle the answer.

B 19

B 20

   A   a square with sides of 2 cm

   B   a rectangle with sides of 2 cm and 4 cm

   C   a regular pentagon with sides of 2 cm

   D   a regular hexagon with sides of 2 cm

1

If $x = 3$ and $y = 4$, find the value of these equations.

B 8

   6 $4y - 3x =$ _____

   7 $9x + 9y =$ _____

   8 $7x - 3y =$ _____

   9 $2x \times y =$ _____

4

10–17 FLATCARE manages a block of flats. It costs between £75 and £220 per week to rent a flat. FLATCARE charges 3% of the rent for their services.

Complete this table.

Rent for the flat	FLATCARE charges	
1 week	4 weeks	52 weeks
£75	_____	_____
£150	_____	_____
£180	_____	_____
£220	_____	_____

What are the **prime factors** of:

18–20 105? _____, _____ and _____

21–23 231? _____, _____ and _____

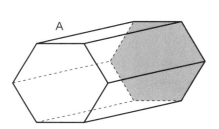

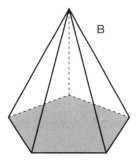

24–26 Shape A has _____ faces, _____ edges and _____ **vertices**.

27–29 Shape B has _____ faces, _____ edges and _____ **vertices**.

Round these numbers to the nearest 100.

30 21 512 _____

31 48 167 _____

32 113 851 _____

33 Which is more: 1 lb or 1 kg of chickpeas? _____

34 Which is less: 60 g or $1\frac{1}{2}$ oz of cannellini beans? _____

35 Which is more: 500 g or 12 oz of lentils? _____

36 Which is less: 10.5 lb or 1.05 kg of red kidney beans? _____

B 3
B 4
B 12
8
B5/B6
6
B 21
6
B 1
3
B 25
B 3

37 To make up a pack of 2.5 kg of dried apricots, how many grams have to be added to 1.03 kg? _____ g

38 There are 37 packs of raisins. Each pack weighs 45 g. How much do all of the packs weigh altogether? _____ kg

Here are the timetables of two trains on the Transpennine railway.

	Train 1	Train 2
Cleethorpes	07:15	16:55
Grimsby Town	07:23	16:46
Habrough	07:33	16:31
Barnetby	07:41	16:22
Scunthorpe	07:56	16:08
Doncaster	08:25 depart 08:27	15:40 depart 15:42
Meadowhall	08:46	15:17
Sheffield	08:54 depart 09:10	15:08 depart 15:11
Stockport	09:51	13:40
Manchester Piccadilly	10:04	14:19
Manchester Airport	10:31	13:56

39 How long does Train 1 take to travel from Cleethorpes to Manchester Airport?

_____

40 How long does Train 2 take to travel from Manchester Airport to Cleethorpes?

_____

Write in hours and / or minutes how long the following journeys take.

41 Habrough to Meadowhall _____

42 Sheffield to Manchester Piccadilly _____

43 Doncaster to Barnetby _____

44 Sheffield to Grimsby Town _____

In a bag of marbles there are 8 cat's eyes for every 5 pearlies. Altogether there are 247 marbles.

45 How many cat's eyes are there? _____

46 How many pearlies are there? _____

Fill in the missing number in each of these calculations.

47 $12 \times 11 \times$ ___ $= 1188$

48 ___ $\times 9 \times 15 = 945$

49 $13 \times 8 \div$ ___ $= 26$

50 $(7 \times 8) \times ($ ___ $+ 4) = 840$

Paper 9

1 $\begin{array}{r} 6817 \\ -\ 948 \\ \hline \end{array}$	**2** $\begin{array}{r} 7008 \\ -\ 4109 \\ \hline \end{array}$	**3** $\begin{array}{r} 16\,835 \\ -\ 8748 \\ \hline \end{array}$	**4** $\begin{array}{r} 23\,642 \\ -\ 15\,863 \\ \hline \end{array}$

Complete these sequences.

5–6 0.125   0.2   0.275   _____   _____

7–8 $8\frac{1}{2}$ $7\frac{3}{4}$ 7   _____   _____

9–10 9.5   12.5   16.5   21.5   _____   _____

11–13 What is the missing number in each of these number squares?

83	76	69
90	A	76
97	90	83

A = _____

117	124	131
110	117	124
B	110	117

B = _____

78	90	C
66	78	90
54	66	78

C = _____

What is $\frac{1}{100}$ of each of these values?

14 2342

15 66.75

16 10.04

17 3.675

18–21 What are the **factors** of 18?

1, _____, _____, _____, _____ and 18

Kitchen scales £8.50

Oven pot £6.40

Cooking tool set £7.99

Can opener £4.75

B 3
B 2

Mrs Perhar is restocking her cooking shop. She buys some of the items shown here. What does she spend on these items?

22 5 kitchen scales £ _____

23 8 oven pots £ _____

24 10 cooking tool sets £ _____

25 12 can openers £ _____

26 How much does Mrs Perhar spend altogether? £ _____

5

27–32 Match the names of these polygons to the shapes by drawing lines between them.

B 18
B 19

Trapezium

Kite

Equilateral triangle

Rhombus

Parallelogram

Pentagon

6

B8/B3
B2/B6

Find the value of x, y and z in these equations.

33 $2y \div 3 = 4$ $y =$ _____

34 $3x + 36 = 45$ $x =$ _____

35 $z^2 = 49$ $z =$ _____

B8/B2
B 4

Now use the values that you have found for x, y and z to solve these equations.

36 $4x + 5y + 3z =$ _____

37 $2x^2 + 3y - z =$ _____

5

38 A ride on the Fear Generator costs £*t* and a ride on the Gut Wrencher costs £*s*. Expressed as an equation, what did Lou spend if he had 6 rides on the Gut Wrencher and 3 rides on the Fear Generator? _____

B 8
1
B 14

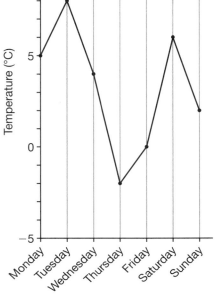

39 What was the temperature on Saturday? _____ °C

40 What was the temperature on Thursday? _____ °C

41 What is the difference between the highest and lowest temperatures in the week? _____ °

3

42–47 Complete this table:

B 20

Perimeter of rectangle	Length = 4 × width	Width
30 cm	_____ cm	_____ cm
50 cm	_____ cm	_____ cm
80 cm	_____ cm	_____ cm

6

B1/B10

48 Write twenty-six thousand, four hundred and four in numbers. _____

49 Write 17 058 in words. _____

50 Write one tenth of four hundred and sixteen in numbers. _____

3

Now go to the Progress Chart to record your score!   **Total**   50

Paper 10

Find the sum of these weights.

1 275 g + 1.5 kg + 320 g =   _____ kg

2 806 g + 2.3 kg + 196 g =   _____ kg

Find the difference in these weights.

3 1.65 kg and 860 g =   _____ kg

4 14.8 kg and 2650 g =   _____ kg

Calculate these divisions, giving the answers in metres.

5 2.2 km ÷ 8 =   _____ m

6 1.33 km ÷ 7 =   _____ m

What are the **coordinates** of:

7 Shaleton?

(_____ , _____)

8 Sandy Bay?

(_____ , _____)

9 Netherton?

(_____ , _____)

What place is located:

10 NE of Speckle Hill?

_____

11 due west of Fresh Harbour?

_____

12 SW of Netherton?

_____

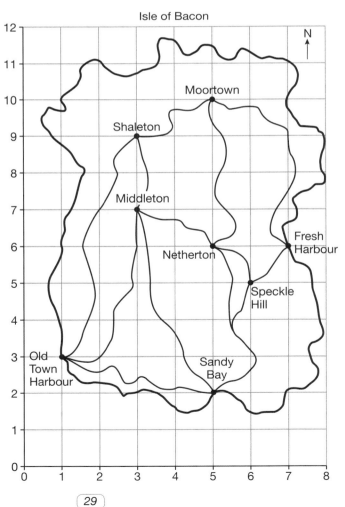

There are two buses on the Isle of Bacon. Here is the morning timetable for one of the buses:

Netherton (out)	09:00
Sandy Bay	09:15
Old Town Harbour	09:35
Middleton	10:00
Shaleton	10:15
Moortown	10:23
Fresh Harbour	10:50
Speckle Hill	11:02
Netherton (return)	11:18

13 How long does it take to travel from Netherton to Old Town Harbour? _____ minutes

14 How long does it take to travel from Old Town Harbour back to Netherton? _____ h _____ min

15 How long does it take to travel from Moortown back to Netherton? _____ minutes

16 If the other bus starts from Netherton at 09:30 and takes the same time to do the same route, what time will it get back? ___ : ___

4

Look at these numbers.

17–19 10   15   20   12   18

What is the **mean**? ___   What is the **median**? ___   What is the **range**? ___

20–22 14   19   27   24   26   13   17

What is the **mean**? ___   What is the **median**? ___   What is the **range**? ___

6

Frances is a salesperson selling laptops and tablets, software and accessories. She gets paid a commission on her sales.

23 On her first £10 000 worth of sales she gets 2% commission. If she makes £10 000 of sales what commission would she get? £ _____

24 On the next £5000 worth of sales she gets 3% commission. How much is that? £ _____

25–27 For any sales above £15 000 Frances gets 5% commission.

Here is a table of her sales for the last three years. How much commission does she get in each year?

	Sales	**Commission**
Year 1	£15 000	£ _____
Year 2	£25 000	£ _____
Year 3	£45 000	£ _____

5

How many lines of symmetry do the following shapes have?

28 An isosceles triangle ___   **29** A regular pentagon ___

30 A **kite** ___   **31** A square ___

32–34 Find-a-place Estate Agents charge a 2% fee on the selling price of a house. What fee did that they charge on these properties?

Selling price	2% fee
£175 000	£_____
£235 000	£_____
£380 000	£_____

Work out these values.

35 one twelfth of 192 ___   **36** one twelfth of 540 ___

37 one twelfth of 996 ___   **38** one twelfth of 1080 ___

39–41 Mia spent a day out birdwatching and made a note of all the birds she saw. At the end of the day she noticed there were 4 starlings to 3 sparrows to 1 robin. If she counted 56 birds altogether, how many were:

starlings? ___   sparrows? ___   robins? ___

In a tropical aquarium there are 8 guppies for every 3 swordtails. There are 121 fish altogether. How many are:

42 guppies? ___

43 swordtails? ___

Round these numbers to the nearest 10.

44 13 126 _____   **45** 29 533 _____   **46** 106 044 _____

Find the answers to these calculations.

47 $\frac{1}{6} + \frac{1}{3} =$ ___   **48** $\frac{3}{10} + \frac{3}{5} =$ ___

49 $12 \times \frac{1}{3} =$ ___   **50** $1\frac{1}{2} + 1\frac{2}{10} =$ ___

Now go to the Progress Chart to record your score! Total 50

Paper 11

The diagram consists of a larger square with a smaller square drawn at its centre.

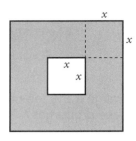

1 What is the area of the shaded part of this shape? _____

Multiply these by 100.

2 60.3 _____   **3** 7.51 _____

Multiply these by 1000.

4 6.03 _____   **5** 12.12 _____   **6** 0.635 _____

A sports outfitter sold 120 T-shirts last week. Here is a pie chart showing the percentage of different colours sold.

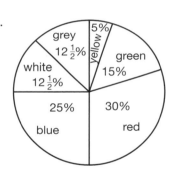

7 How many grey T-shirts were sold? _____

8 How many red T-shirts were sold? _____

9 How many white and green T-shirts were sold altogether? _____

10 How many more blue than yellow T-shirts were sold? _____

Put one number from column A and one number from column B into each of these statements to make them true.

A	B
$\frac{4}{3}$	0.09
7.01	$\frac{3}{50}$
10%	$\sqrt{36}$

11–12 _____ < 7 < _____

13–14 _____ < 0.7 < _____

15–16 _____ < 0.07 < _____

Josie is a scientist who counts tree rings to see how old the trees are. Each ring represents one year of the tree's life. She looked at an oak tree that was three times as old as an ash tree that was twice as old as a sycamore tree. She counted 540 rings altogether.

B 13

17 How old was the sycamore? _____ years

18 How old was the ash? _____ years

19 How old was the oak? _____ years

3

B 14
B 27

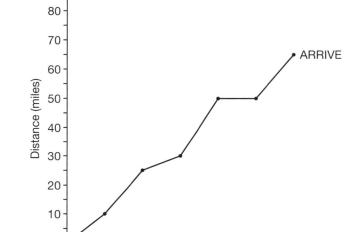

This is a distance–time graph. It shows how far I drove my car the other day, and how long I drove for.

20 How long did my journey take? ___ hours

21 How long was my car stationary? ___ hours

22–23 Between which times was I travelling the fastest? ___ : ___ and ___ : ___

4

Jed Irongrip plays professional golf. In a recent tournament he played four rounds of golf. Here are the scores for three of the rounds. What did he get in the fourth round?

B 15

24 69   72   69   ___   **Mean** average score: 71

The winner of the tournament was Blaise Fairway. He beat Jed by 8 shots (so he scored a total of 8 hits less).

25 What was Blaise's mean average score? _____

2

Calculate these amounts of money.

26 49p + 37p + 18p = £ _____

27 £4.30 × 30 = £ _____

28 £15.20 + 88p + £1.75 = £ _____

29 £90.31 × 6 = £ _____

30 £34.50 ÷ 23 = £ _____

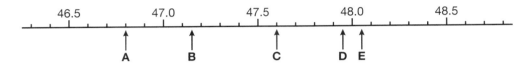

Which numbers are the arrows are pointing to on this number line?

31 Arrow A _____

32 Arrow B _____

33 Arrow C _____

34 Arrow D _____

35 Arrow E _____

Adhesive tape

£1.29

Scissors

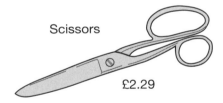

£2.29

Stapler

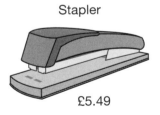

£5.49

Rubber bands

£1.59

Box of staples

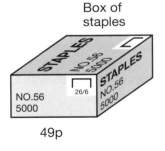

49p

The school secretary is buying some things for the school office. Work out what she spent on these items.

36 Three rolls of adhesive tape. £ _____

37 Two pairs of scissors. £ _____

38 A stapler and two boxes of staples. £ _____

39 Three boxes of rubber bands. £ _____

40 How much did she spend altogether? £ _____

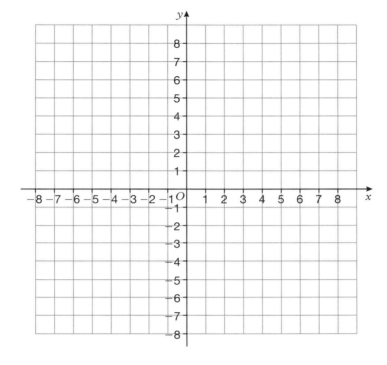

41–43 Mark in the **coordinates** (2, −3), (−1, 7) and (−4, −3).

44 Draw in the shape you have mapped.

45 What is the shape called? _____

46 What is the **coordinate** of the point that lies halfway along the line of symmetry? (___ , ___)

Underline the correct answer for each of these calculations.

47 16 × 12 = 129 291 192 162

48 0.25 × 6 = 15 1.5 0.15 1.05 0.105

49 1.2 × 1.2 = 144 14.4 1.044 0.144 1.44

50 27 − 16.9 = 1.01 10.1 11 9.9 0.11

Paper 12

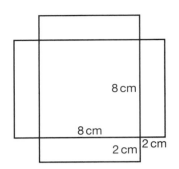

B 21
B 22

1 This is the net of an open box used to pack chocolates. If the chocolates are 0.5 cm tall, work out how many layers of chocolates can be put into the box. ____

2 What is the volume of the box? _____

2

3 A river is 10 km long. How long will it be on a map with a scale of 1:100 000?

_____ cm

B 25
B 26
1

4 Stan is counting his cows. He realises that every third cow is brown and every fourth cow has horns. If Stan has a herd of 36 cows, work out how many are brown with horns. _____

B3/B5
1

Complete these sequences.

5–6 3   4   6   7   9   __   __

7–8 0.85   0.75   0.65   __   __

B 7
4

A temperature sensor was connected to a laptop in a classroom. The temperature in the room was recorded every half an hour during the morning. This is a line graph showing temperature and the time.

B 14

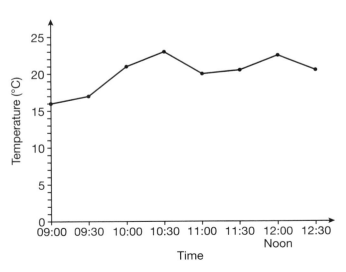

Any answer that requires units of measurement should be marked wrong if the correct units have not been included.

Paper 1

1. 200 020
2. 49 049
3. 5
4. ÷
5. ÷
6. +
7. −
8. −
9. −
10. ×
11–14. $(^-6, ^-3)$, $(^-3, 4)$, $(3, 4)$, $(6, ^-3)$
15. Trapezium
16. 38
17. 46
18. $\frac{1}{3}$ of 8
19. $\frac{1}{6}$
20. $\frac{17}{40}$
21. $\frac{1}{4}$
22. 0.0507
23. $\frac{1}{4}$
24. $\frac{1}{8}$
25. 25%
26. 84
27. 36
28. 24
29. 6
30. 6
31. 7
32. 15
33. 18
34. 18
35. 147
36. 237
37. 357
38. 467
39. $5p + 2q$
40. 100.6
41. 2.65
42. 1.388
43. 4.0615
44. 60°
45. 150°
46. 30°
47. 120°
48. 5
49. 10
50. 25

Paper 2

1. 1677
2. 3384
3. 221
4. 15 165
5. 5615
6. 1306
7. 10.7
8. 31.26
9. 4.585
10. 0.1173
11. C (Red)
12. E (Green)
13. $\frac{1}{2}$
14. $\frac{1}{6}$
15. $\frac{1}{3}$
16. 25
17. B
18. E
19. 01:32
20. 16:20
21. 17:37
22. 13:25
23. 14:42
24. 23:15
25. 7.5
26. 9.05
27. 6.1
28. 8.18
29. ÷
30. +
31. −
32. C
33. 10
34. 30
35. 40
36–39.

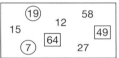

40. 17
41. 77
42. 36
43. 0.5
44. 4
45. 115
46. 80
47. 75
48. 44
49. 96
50. 25 miles

Paper 3

1. 15 cm²
2. 12 cm²
3. 6 cm²
4. 12 cm²
5. 28 cm
6–11.

Price	Price rise	Total price
£20	**£2.50**	**£22.50**
£50	**£6.25**	**£56.25**
£100	**£12.50**	**£112.50**

12. 8
13. 4
14. 9
15. 5
16. 9
17. 18
18. 27
19. 16
20. 17
21. 36
22. 37
23. 5 cm²
24. $7\frac{1}{2}$ cm² or 7.5 cm²
25. 14 cm²
26. 12 cm²
27. 580
28. 740
29. 1500
30. 2400
31. 24 000
32. 80 000
33–37.

Leave Craggytown	Leave Sandyville
9:00 a.m.	**9:28** a.m.
9:52 a.m.	**10:20** a.m.
10:44 a.m.	**11:12** a.m.

38. 9 m 81 cm
39. 3 m 98 cm
40. 38 m 50 cm
41. 3 kg 850 g
42. 2 kg 560 g
43–44. Soap powder, scouring pads
45. 9.95
46. 14.74
47. £9.69
48. £16.29
49. £18.75
50. £87.36

Paper 4

1. $\frac{1}{6}$
2. $\frac{1}{6}$
3. $\frac{1}{2}$
4. $\frac{1}{3}$
5. 8.34
6. 8.38
7. 8.46
8. 8.52
9. 3
10. 5
11. 3
12. 4
13. 18 cm²
14. 2 cm²
15. 4 cm²
16. 48 cm²
17.
```
    5 1 7 5
    3 9 2 7
+   2 6 4 1
  ---------
  1 1 7 4 3
```
18.
```
  1 6 8 3
 -  8 5 9
  -------
    8 2 4
```

ANSWERS

19
$$456 \times 5 = 2280$$

20 44 mm
21 70 mm²
22 0.0165
23 0.00483
24 0.003217
25 0.000791
26 22
27 19
28 29.75
29 22.5
30 22.75
31 20
32 29
33 29
34 26
35 30
36 0.0625
37 3.68
38 0.79
39 37
40 48
41 27
42 2.173
43 0.546
44 0.0189
45 17:11
46 5:11 p.m.
47 10:15
48 10:15 a.m.
49 23:03
50 11:03 p.m.

Paper 5

1 69
2 Spain
3 30
4 21
5 75
6 11:14
7 10:26
8 16
9 8
10 37
11 33
12 112
13 224
14 66
15 220
16 374
17 280.50
18 445.50
19 6 cm²
20 14 cm²
21 18 cm²
22 22.5 cm²
23 12.5 cm²
24 26 cm²

25 28 cm²
26 60 cm²
27 73
28 4350
29 200
30 19 200
31 40.50
32 FALSE
33 FALSE
34 TRUE
35 TRUE
36 TRUE
37 FALSE

38–41

28   (37)   102
(5)
(19)   121
56   16   (29)   99

42 1.897
43 23.873
44 0.632
45 400
46 2
47 800 000
48 15%
49 80 000
50 500 000

Paper 6

1 4400
2 4300
3 4000
4 3600
5 3200
6 2800
7 >
8 <
9 =
10 <
11 =
12 >
13 59
14 116
15 167
16 $\frac{1}{2}$
17 $\frac{1}{10}$
18 $\frac{2}{5}$
19 0
20 A = 120
21 B = 60
22 C = 40
23 D = 58
24 852 ml
25 4 l 544 ml
26 1 l 988 ml
27 6 l 248 ml
28 9004
29 97
30 19.5

31 19
32 32
33 3.9
34 +
35 ÷
36 ×
37 ÷
38 +
39 −
40 3.65 m
41 156.78 m
42 $2x^2$
43–45 2, 3, 7
46 36
47 28
48 558
49 72
50 45

Paper 7

1 18 m
2 64 000
3 129 000
4 28
5 2
6 3.50
7 $4\frac{2}{3}$
8 $6\frac{1}{3}$
9 $3\frac{2}{3}$
10 $2\frac{3}{5}$
11 $10\frac{2}{5}$
12 $3\frac{1}{20}$
13 $7\frac{3}{4}$
14 9.55
15 5
16 0.8
17 30
18 36
19 Obtuse
20 Reflex
21 Right-angled
22 Acute
23 6
24 12
25 24
26 30
27 6
28 28
29 16
30 92.6
31 1.48
32 2.729
33 36 m²
34 60 m²
35 24 m
36 32 m
37 81
38 7^2

39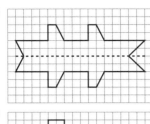

40

41 £22 575
42 £19 350
43 £20 425
44 £22 037.50
45 9:00
46 3
47 63 000 km²
48 60 000 km²
49 58 000 km²
50 31 000 km²

Paper 8

1 6877
2 7980
3 78
4 221
5 C
6 7
7 63
8 9
9 24

10–17

Rent for the flat	FLATCARE charges	
1 week	4 weeks	52 weeks
£75	**£9**	**£117**
£150	**£18**	**£234**
£180	**£21.60**	**£280.80**
£220	**£26.40**	**£343.20**

18–20 3, 5, 7
21–23 3, 7, 11
24 8
25 18
26 12
27 6
28 10
29 6
30 21 500
31 48 200
32 113 900
33 1 kg
34 $1\frac{1}{2}$ oz
35 500 g
36 1.05 kg

37 1470
38 1.665
39 3 h 16 min
40 2 h 59 min
41 1 h 13 min
42 54 min
43 40 min
44 1 h 35 min
45 152
46 95
47 9
48 7
49 4
50 11

Paper 9

1 5869
2 2899
3 8087
4 7779
5 0.35
6 0.425
7 $6\frac{1}{4}$
8 $5\frac{1}{2}$
9 27.5
10 34.5
11 83
12 103
13 102
14 23.42
15 0.6675
16 0.1004
17 0.03675
18 2
19 3
20 6
21 9
22 42.50
23 £51.20
24 79.90
25 57.00
26 £230.60
27–32
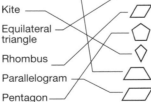
Trapezium
Kite
Equilateral triangle
Rhombus
Parallelogram
Pentagon
33 6
34 3
35 7
36 63
37 29
38 $6s + 3t$
39 6
40 ⁻2
41 10

42–47

Perimeter	Length = 4 × width	Width
30 cm	**12** cm	**3** cm
50 cm	**20** cm	**5** cm
80 cm	**32** cm	**8** cm

48 26 404
49 Seventeen thousand and fifty-eight
50 41.6

Paper 10

1 2.095
2 3.302
3 0.79
4 12.15
5 275
6 190
7 (3, 9)
8 (5, 2)
9 (5, 6)
10 Fresh Harbour
11 Netherton
12 Old Town Harbour
13 35
14 1 hr 43 minutes
15 55
16 11:48
17 15
18 15
19 10
20 20
21 19
22 14
23 200
24 150
25 350
26 850
27 1850
28 1
29 5
30 1
31 4
32 3500
33 4700
34 7600
35 16
36 45
37 83
38 90
39 28
40 21
41 7
42 88
43 33
44 13 130
45 29 530
46 106 040
47 $\frac{3}{6}$ or $\frac{1}{2}$

48 $\frac{9}{10}$
49 4
50 $2\frac{7}{10}$

Paper 11

1 $8x^2$
2 6030
3 751
4 6030
5 12120
6 635
7 15
8 36
9 33
10 24
11–12 $\sqrt{36} < 7 < 7.01$
13–14 $0.09 < 0.7 < \frac{4}{3}$
15–16 $\frac{3}{50} < 0.07 < 10\%$
17 60
18 120
19 360
20 3
21 0.5
22 11:30
23 12:00
24 74
25 69
26 1.04
27 129
28 17.83
29 541.86
30 1.50
31 46.8
32 47.15
33 47.6
34 47.95
35 48.05
36 3.87
37 4.58
38 6.47
39 4.77
40 19.69
41–44

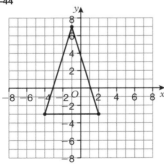

45 Isosceles triangle
46 ($^-$1, 2)
47 192
48 1.5
49 1.44
50 10.1

Paper 12

1 4
2 128 cm³
3 10
4 3
5 10
6 12
7 0.55
8 0.45
9 16°C
10 9:00 a.m.
11 23°C
12 10:30 a.m.
13 The children went out to play and left the door open.
14 28
15 6
16 28
17 27
18 180
19 30
20 25
21 5
22 10
23 64
24 34
25 36
26 11^2
27 8
28 16
29 24
30 $\frac{5}{10}$
31 $\frac{6}{12}$
32 $\frac{4}{12}$
33 $\frac{5}{15}$
34 $\frac{4}{20}$
35 $\frac{5}{25}$
36 73
37 101
38 63
39 100 m
40 600 m²
41 80 m
42 400 m²
43 60 m
44 200 m²
45 180 m
46 3180 kg
47 3161 kg
48 3555 kg
49 9896 kg
50 1060 kg

Paper 13

1 97
2 0.097
3 400
4 4
5 6.75

6 0.675
7 11.5
8 0.115
9 19
10 0.019
11 3
12 13
13 21
14 42
15 17
16–21 Forward 3, Right 90°, Forward 2, Left 90°, Forward 4, Right 90°, Forward 2
22 166.50
23 0.65
24 27.45
25 26
26 3 packs
27 27 cm²
28 47.05
29 0.22
30 12.55
31 42
32 56
33 14
34 5
35 8
36 9
37 10
38–40

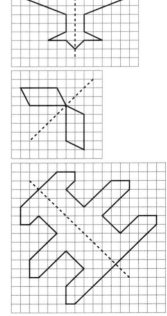

41 80
42 18
43 24
44 10
45 10.07

A4

46 23.75
47 28.50
48 15.47
49 1.70
50 9.01

Paper 14

1 30°
2 20°
3 40°
4 12:12
5 12:38
6 12:53
7 13:11
8 13:44
9 54.4
10 5.37
11 9.75
12 500
13 39p
14 30p
15 45p
16 15
17 30
18 75
19 18
20 20
21 36
22 77
23 52
24 144
25–31

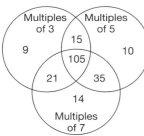

32 $p - 8$
33 276.19
34 $1832\frac{3}{5}$
35 4.5
36 38 915
37 33.02
38 60.80
39 1.70
40 42.90
41 3
42 4
43 6
44 60
45 167 ⎫
46 122 ⎪
47 59 ⎬ Answers are correct to
48 100 ⎪ within 2° of these
49 5   ⎪
50 20 ⎭

Paper 15

1 179
2 3.87
3 77
4 10.15
5 714
6 679
7 16
8 18
9 13.00
10 13.25
11 $\frac{1}{32}$
12 $\frac{1}{64}$
13 26
14 31
15–20

	Length	Width	Perimeter	Area
Rectangle 1	6 cm	4 cm	**20** cm	**24** cm²
Rectangle 2	9 cm	**3** cm	24 cm	**27** cm²
Rectangle 3	**11** cm	6 cm	**34** cm	66 cm²

21 10
22 75
23 50
24 250
25 8
26 19
27 6
28 110
29 9
30 34
31 $20y^2$
32 40%
33 15%
34 $\frac{1}{5}$
35 $\frac{1}{4}$
36 16
37–38 17, 31
39 Iris Parker
40 Sandy Young
41 Bob and Sally Macintosh
42 (7, 4)
43 (2, 2)
44 Bob and Sally Macintosh
45 20
46 30
47 60
48–50 B, D, F

Paper 16

1 2
2 3
3 5
4 2
5 5

6 11
7 3
8 5
9 11
10 $8x$
11 53
12 $\frac{7}{21}$
13 20%
14 1.9
15 27
16 3.5
17 10.1
18 0.659
19 0.038
20 0.00165
21 4
22 2
23 $\frac{1}{2}$
24 $\frac{1}{4}$
25 $1\frac{1}{3}$
26 1
27 12
28 3
29 21
30 12
31 38
32 13
33 28
34 6
35 3.12
36 7.45
37 4.94
38 33p
39 58
40 24
41 20
42 54
43–46 78%, $\frac{2}{3}$, $\frac{17}{50}$, 23%
47 Square-based pyramid
48 Cuboid
49 Tetrahedron
50 Open-topped cube

Paper 17

1 22.8
2 64.68
3 60.8
4 42.55
5 34
6 190
7 3.2
8 23
9 $<$
10 $=$
11 $>$
12 $=$
13 $<$
14 50
15 75
16 150

17 30
18 400
19 60
20 6
21 8
22 3
23 48
24 28
25 18
26 18
27 24
28 22
29 One hundred and seventy-two
30 Five hundred and seventy
31 Thirty-nine
32 One hundred and eighty-five point five
33 240
34 $\frac{1}{20}$
35 $\frac{9}{20}$
36 20%
37 30%
38 22
39 18
40 2
41 106
42 61
43 10 cm²
44 15 cm²
45 14 cm
46 22 cm
47 15
48 6
49 9
50 18

Paper 18

1 12
2 15
3 198
4 4
5 96
6 9
7 4
8 35
9 7
10 16 m
11 16 m²
12 24 cm²
13 48 cm³
14 12
15 22:00
16 19:30
17 11
18 18:15
19 2
20 25
21 8
22 10:05
23 94

24 54
25 88
26 2088
27 32
28 24
29 $\frac{1}{12}$
30 $\frac{1}{6}$
31 $\frac{5}{12}$
32 $\frac{1}{4}$
33 19
34 25
35 32
36 23

37–41

	Wholesale price	Profit (40%)	Shop price
Item 1	£6.25	£2.50	**£8.75**
Item 2	£8.50	**£3.40**	**£11.90**
Item 3	£12.75	**£5.10**	**£17.85**

42 23.20
43 58
44 348
45 870
46 15
47 81
48 1.25 or $1\frac{1}{4}$
49 10.75
50 4.5

Paper 19

1 3
2 11
3 57
4 108
5 3
6 D
7 2
8 ÷
9 >
10 =
11 50
12 10
13 40
14 30
15 22

16–21

	Bill	Surcharge	New bill
Mr Watt	£320	**£24**	**£344**
Ms Bright	£420	**£31.50**	**£451.50**
Mrs Brass	£472	**£35.40**	**£507.40**

22 9.22
23 1.21
24 2.436
25 170
26 9000 cm²
27 120 cm
28 3600 cm²

29 480 cm
30 $2\frac{7}{20}$
31 $8\frac{1}{3}$
32 $9\frac{1}{3}$
33 $43\frac{1}{2}$
34 0.48
35 0.25
36 0.2
37 0.125

38–43

×	3	6	7
2	6	12	14
4	12	24	28
8	24	48	56

44 TRUE
45 FALSE
46 TRUE
47 TRUE

48–50

Values					Mean of values
6	12	**9**	8	10	9
15	17	13	19	**21**	17
21	25	29	23	27	**25**

Paper 20

1 43.05
2 43.8
3 42.37
4 43.49
5–8 42.37, 43.05, 43.49, 43.8
9 $n + 5$
10 20.32
11 34
12 36
13 70
14 36
15 21
16 9
17 42

18–21

	Odd	Even
Square number	9	36
Not a square number	21	42

22 37
23 8

24–29

Bucket of water — 1 kg
Height of a man — 200 km
Packet of sweets — 5 litres
Distance from london to Birmingham — 300 ml
Liquid in a bowl of soup — 1 m 80 cm
Weight of bag of sugar — 100 g

30 96
31 128
32 128
33 Radio 5
34 6:30 a.m.
35 9:15 p.m.
36 1:12 a.m.
37 11:59 p.m.
38 2:06 p.m.
39 5:23 p.m.
40 138.60
41 139
42 390.40
43 390
44 55.26
45 55
46 0.496
47 0.036
48 0.0111
49 0.00376
50 0.00052

Paper 21

1 1
2 250
3 499
4 14.95
5 15.15
6 15.75
7 16.05
8 7p
9 7p
10 66p
11 $7\frac{1}{8}$
12 $4\frac{6}{7}$
13 $5\frac{1}{9}$
14 24
15 24
16 70
17 30

18–23

	Length	Width	Area	Perimeter
Rectangle 1	13 cm	6 cm	**78** cm²	**38** cm
Rectangle 2	**12** cm	7 cm	84 cm²	**38** cm
Rectangle 3	9 cm	**5** cm	45 cm²	**28** cm

24 71
25 12
26 6
27 24
28 3.285
29 3.16
30 42.975
31 (4, 3)
32 Lower Pasture
33 (1, 3)

34 Little Copse
35 (6, 6)
36 7
37 18
38 16
39 15
40 8
41 $4\frac{1}{4}$
42 6 tenths
43 6 units
44 6 tens
45 6 thousands

46–50

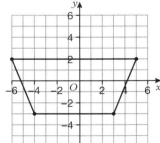

Paper 22

1–6

	To nearest 1000	To nearest 10 000	To nearest 100 000
163 712	164 000	160 000	200 000
349 493	349 000	350 000	300 000

7 168
8 50
9 45
10 58.5
11 1.519
12 22.06
13 49.5
14 965

15–18

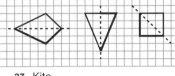

19 Trapezium
20 1
21 24
22 60
23 12
24 33
25 £3.37
26 £1.41
27 £14.97
28 £10.07
29 150
30 36%
31 18%
32 24%
33 40%

34–36

37 Kite
38 Isosceles triangle
39 Square

40–45

Sweet	Starting number	Sweets shared	Sweets remaining
Tom thumb drops	252	**112**	**140**
Micro mints	495	**220**	**275**
Tiny tots	369	**164**	**205**

46 135
47 225
48 270
49 $\frac{3}{8}$
50 $\frac{3}{4}$

Paper 23

1 994.3
2 13.1
3 785.9
4 861.9
5 17
6 18
7 57
8 18

9–14

	Wholesale price	15%	Shop price
Book A	£6.80	**£1.02**	**£7.82**
Book B	£8.00	**£1.20**	**£9.20**
Book C	£10.60	**£1.59**	**£12.19**

15	14:59	**27**	84	**39**	512.5
16	15:01	**28**	16	**40**	305.9
17	15:04	**29**	1050	**41**	1727.1
18	15:21	**30**	$17\frac{1}{2}$	**42**	30 m³
19	15:35	**31**	989.1	**43**	5
20	16:10	**32**	$1\frac{1}{2}$	**44**	1.3
21	0.9	**33**	0.25	**45**	6
22	0.28	**34**	54 cm²	**46**	25
23	0.55	**35**	50 cm²	**47**	2
24	0.375	**36**	96 cm²	**48**	1
25	98	**37**	98 cm²	**49**	25
26	6	**38**	2053.8	**50**	16

9 What was the coolest temperature? _____

10 What time was it at its coolest? Remember to include a.m. or p.m. _____

11 What was the warmest temperature? _____

12 What time was it at its warmest? Remember to include a.m. or p.m. _____

13 Put a tick next to the most likely explanation of the temperature change between 10:30 and 11:00.

☐ The sun came out.

☐ The children went out to play and left the door open.

☐ The teacher turned the heaters on.

☐ There was a total eclipse of the Sun.

5

Mr Asif made a note of the number of children who were in his science class each day for a week.

B 15

Monday	Tuesday	Wednesday	Thursday	Friday
23	28	27	28	29

14 What is the **mode** number of children? _____

15 What is the **range**? _____

16 What is the **median**? _____

17 What is the **mean**? _____

4

Marina did a survey in her school asking students which sport was their favourite. The numbers for each sport are shown in this pie chart:

B 2

B 12

B 14

Pie chart: Rounders; Cricket 9; Cross-country 45; Football 54; Netball 54; (Rounders 18)

18 How many students did she ask altogether? _____

19 What percentage of the students chose netball? ___ %

20 What percentage of the students chose cross-country? ___ %

21 What percentage of the students chose rounders? ___ %

22 What percentage of the students chose cricket? ___ %

5

Solve these calculations.

23 $8^2 =$ _____

24 $5^2 + 3^2 =$ _____

25 $(2 \times 3) \times (2 \times 3) =$ _____

26 What is 121 written as a square number? _____

27–29 What numbers come out of this machine?

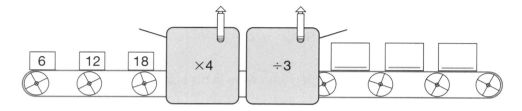

Complete these sequences.

30–31 $\frac{1}{2}$ $\frac{2}{4}$ $\frac{3}{6}$ $\frac{4}{8}$ ___   ___

32–33 $\frac{1}{3}$ $\frac{2}{6}$ $\frac{3}{9}$ ___   ___

34–35 $\frac{1}{5}$ $\frac{2}{10}$ $\frac{3}{15}$ ___   ___

36–38 What is the missing number in each of these number squares?

62	73	84
51	62	A
40	51	62

A = _____

119	128	137
110	119	128
B	110	119

B = _____

33	48	C
18	33	48
3	18	33

C = _____

At the local showground spaces were pegged out for people to put up their stalls and marquees. Here is a plan of one part of the showground:

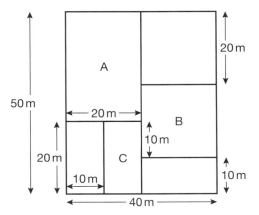

39 What is the perimeter of space A? _____

40 What is the area of space A? _____

41 What is the perimeter of space B? _____

42 What is the area of space B? _____

43 What is the perimeter of space C? _____

44 What is the area of space C? _____

45 What is the perimeter of the whole showground? _____ **7**

A car transporter has three decks, and there are three cars on each deck.

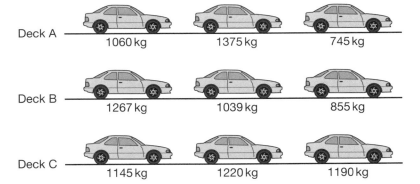

Deck A 1060 kg 1375 kg 745 kg

Deck B 1267 kg 1039 kg 855 kg

Deck C 1145 kg 1220 kg 1190 kg

46 What is the weight of the cars on Deck A? _____

47 What is the weight of the cars on Deck B? _____

48 What is the weight of the cars on Deck C? _____

49 What is the total weight of the cars? _____

50 What is the **mean** average weight of cars on Deck A? _____ **5**

Now go to the Progress Chart to record your score! Total **50**

Paper 13

Find the answers to these calculations.

1 $(9 \times 8) + 25 =$ _____

2 What is this answer divided by 1000? _____

3 $(11 \times 35) + 15 =$ _____

4 What is this answer divided by 100? _____

5 $(125 \div 20) + 0.50 =$ _____

6 What is this answer divided by 10? _____

7 $(35 \div 7) + 6.5 =$ _____

8 What is this answer divided by 100? _____

9 $(264 \div 22) + 7 =$ _____

10 What is this answer divided by 1000? _____

Fill in the missing numbers.

11 $(8 \times$ ___ $) + 17 = 41$

12 $32 = ($ ___ $\times 2) + 6$

13 $3 \times (56 -$ ___ $) = 105$

14 $0.5 \times (8 +$ ___ $) = 25$

15 $165 = 5 \times (16 +$ ___ $)$

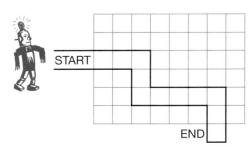

16–21 The robot is on START. Describe the route the robot must take to get to the END. The robot can only move Forward, Turn Right 90° and Turn Left 90°. The first instruction has been done for you:

Forward 3, _____

_____

Janice's dad is making it easier for her to do her homework by providing her with a workspace. Work out the answers to these decisions and choices.

22 Dad pays for the computer in three equal instalments. The computer costs £499.50. How much is each instalment?   £ _____

23 He buys a lamp for £17.75, a wastepaper bin for £6.50, a pencil pot for £2.95 and a paper tray for £2.15. How much change will he get from £30? £ _____

24 Dad also buys a work trolley for £59.90. For this he pays a £5 deposit and then the remaining amount in two instalments. How much is each instalment? £ _____

25 Janice is saving for a printer costing £79. She saves £1.50 a week for 7 weeks, then £2.50 a week for 17 weeks. How much more does she need to save? £ _____

26 DVD disk packs are £5.99 and black printer cartridges are £8.45. Janice has £35. She buys two printer cartridges. How many disk packs can she buy? _____

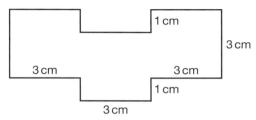

27 What is the area of this shape? _____

Underline the correct answer to each of these calculations.

28 46.3 + 0.75 =	40.75	40.57	47.05	47.50	47.55
29 0.05 + 0.17 =	2.2	0.22	0.022	0.202	2.02
30 9.2 + 3.1 + 0.25 =	1.255	125.5	1255	0.1255	12.55

Out of 112 children's party bags, $\frac{7}{8}$ have a moving toy inside. Of these, $\frac{3}{7}$ are jumping beetles and the rest are creeping snakes.

31 How many contain beetles? _____

32 How many contain snakes? _____

33 How many contain neither? _____

Zak has entered a quiz. If he answers every question correctly, his score (which is 1 for the first question) is doubled each time.

34 How many questions does Zak need to answer correctly to get a total of 16 points? _____

35 How many questions does Zak need to answer correctly to get a total of 128 points? _____

36 How many questions does Zak need to answer correctly to get a total of 256 points? _____

37 How many questions does Zak need to answer correctly to get a total of 512 points? _____

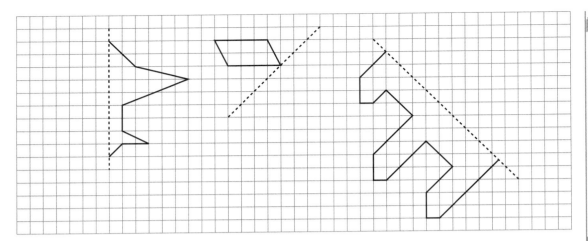

38–40 The dashed lines are mirror lines. Draw in the reflected shapes.

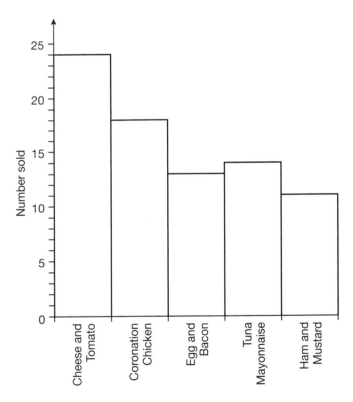

3

This bar chart shows the sales of sandwiches one morning in a local sandwich shop.

41 How many sandwiches were sold altogether? _____

42 How many coronation chicken were sold? _____

43 How many egg and bacon, and ham and mustard were sold altogether? _____

44 How many more cheese and tomato than tuna mayonnaise were sold? _____

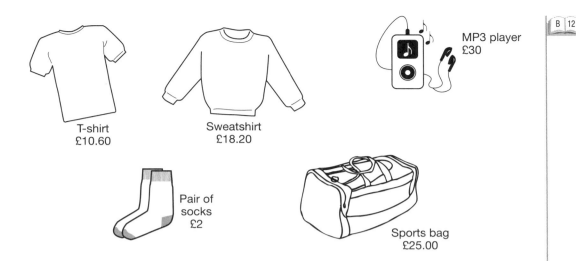

T-shirt
£10.60

Sweatshirt
£18.20

MP3 player
£30

Pair of
socks
£2

Sports bag
£25.00

Here are the prices of five articles in a local sports outfitter.
If there was a discount of 5%, what would the prices be for the items listed below?

45 One t-shirt £ _____

46 One sports bag £ _____

47 One MP3 player £ _____

3

If there was a discount of 15%, what would the price be for each of these items?

B 12

48 One sweatshirt £ _____

49 One pair of socks £ _____

50 One t-shirt £ _____

3

Now go to the Progress Chart to record your score! **Total** 50

Paper 14

1–3 Work out the values of x, y and z in these triangles. Remember that the angles of a triangle always total 180°.

B 3

B 18

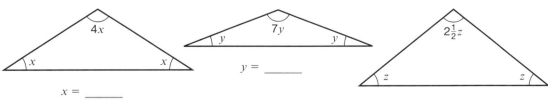

$4x$

x x

$x =$ _____

$7y$

y y

$y =$ _____

$2\frac{1}{2}z$

z z

$z =$ _____

3

4–8 Fill in this timetable for Bus B using the timings for parts of the journey of Bus A to help you. Times should be written as 24-hour clock times.

B 27

	Bus A	Bus B
Pondtown	10:35	11:40
Wyeville	11:07	__ : __
Avonmead	11:33	__ : __
Severnlea	11:48	__ : __
Wyeford	12:06	__ : __
Pondtown	12:39	__ : __

5

9 Thami bought a length of cord that measured 3 m in length. He used 1.02 m, 67 cm, 41 cm, 8.9 cm and then 26.7 cm of the cord.

How much of the cord was left? _____ cm

B25/B1
B2/B4

10 Jo French's washing line stretches three times across her backyard. It takes 16.11 m of line to do this.

How far is it across the backyard? _____ m

B1/B3

2

A litre bottle of KERPOW washing-up liquid costs £1.95.

B3/B5

11 How much would a five-litre bottle of KERPOW cost? £ _____

12 If I use 10 ml to wash my pots each time, how many pot washes can I do from a five-litre bottle before I need a new one? _____

13 How much will 20 pot washes cost ? _____ p

3

KERPOW is also sold in 500 ml and 250 ml bottles. They cost £1.05 and 60p respectively.

B2/B3

14 How much more would it cost me to buy four 500 ml bottles than two 1-litre bottles? _____ p

15 How much more would it cost me to buy four 250 ml bottles rather than a litre bottle? _____ p

2

At the local fire station they have different lengths of fire hose. The shortest is half the length of the middle-sized one, and one fifth of the length of the longest one. If I connect the three different hose lengths together I make a hose 120 m long.

B 13

16 How long is the shortest hose? _____ m

17 How long is the middle hose? _____ m

18 How long is the longest hose? _____ m

3

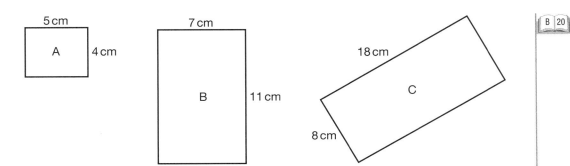

Calculate the perimeter and area of each of these rectangles.

19–20 Rectangle A has a perimeter of _____ cm, and an area of _____ cm².

21–22 Rectangle B has a perimeter of _____ cm, and an area of _____ cm².

23–24 Rectangle C has a perimeter of _____ cm, and an area of _____ cm².

25–31 Write these numbers in the appropriate sections of this Venn diagram.

9	35	10	105
14	15	21	

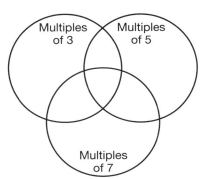

32 If Naveen is p years old in 2 years' time what was her age 6 years ago? _____ years

Find the answers to these calculations.

33 $496.07 - 219.88 =$ _____

34 $1792\frac{1}{2} + 40\frac{1}{10} =$ _____

35 $31.5 \div 7 =$ _____

36 $905 \times 43 =$ _____

Calculate these amounts of money.

37 $503p + £27.99 =$ £ _____

38 $£7.60 \times 8 =$ £ _____

39 $\frac{1}{8}$ of £13.60 = £ _____

40 $£43.05 - 15p =$ £ _____

Work out what number the letter represents in each of these equations.

41 $6a + 7 = 25$ $a =$ ____

42 $3b \times 6 = 72$ $b =$ ____

43 $8c \div 4 = 12$ $c =$ ____

Now use the values you have found for *a*, *b* and *c* to find the solution to this equation.

44 $(5a \times 2b) - 10c =$ ____

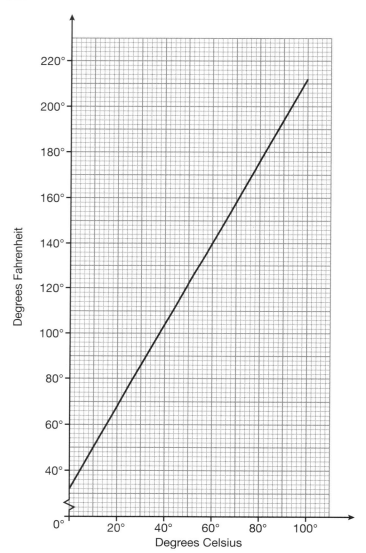

Use this temperature conversion graph to convert these temperatures.

45 75 °C → _____ °F   **46** 50 °C → _____ °F

47 15 °C → _____ °F   **48** 212 °F → _____ °C

49 41 °F → _____ °C   **50** 68 °F → _____ °C

Paper 15

Solve these calculations, writing your answers as numbers.

B1/B2

1 Add one hundred and five to seventy-four. _____

B 3

2 What is the sum of two point five two and one point three five? _____

3 Find the difference between three hundred and seventy-five and two hundred and ninety-eight. _____

4 Subtract fifteen point nine seven from twenty-six point one two. _____

5 Multiply eleven point nine by sixty. _____

6 What are seventy lots of nine point seven? _____

7 How many twelves go into one hundred and ninety-two? _____

8 Divide four hundred and fourteen by twenty-three. _____ **8**

Complete these sequences.

B 7

9–10 12.25 12.50 12.75 ____ ____

11–12 $\frac{1}{2}$ $\frac{1}{4}$ $\frac{1}{8}$ $\frac{1}{16}$ ____ ____

13–14 16   17   19   22   ____ ____ **6**

15–20 Fill in the missing values in this table of different-sized rectangles.

B 20

	Length	Width	Perimeter	Area
Rectangle 1	6 cm	4 cm	_____ cm	_____ cm²
Rectangle 2	9 cm	_____ cm	24 cm	_____ cm²
Rectangle 3	_____ cm	6 cm	_____ cm	66 cm²

6

21–24 In my local travel shop I can exchange euros for British pounds when I come back from holiday. I get £1 for every 1.46 euros. Complete this table for different values of euros that people exchanged in front of me in the shop.

B3/B13

Euros	Pounds
€14.60	£_____
€109.50	£_____
€73	£_____
€365	£_____

4

47

Calculate the **mean** and **range** of each of these sets of numbers.

25–26 22   15   18   23   17   Range _____ Mean _____

27–28 106   112   110   112   Range _____ Mean _____

29–30 36   29   35   38   36   30   Range _____ Mean _____

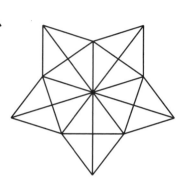

31 If each of the small triangles shown has an area of y^2, what is the area of the star?   _____

Mrs Tilley keeps a variety of poultry. This pie chart shows the numbers of each kind:

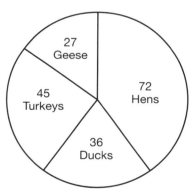

32 What percentage of the poultry are hens?   _____ %

33 What percentage of the poultry are geese?   _____ %

34 What fraction of the poultry are ducks?   _____

35 What fraction of the poultry are turkeys?   _____

Here are some of the numbers that were picked out of the bag at a bingo evening.

  20   32   95   16   18   31   24   17

36 Which of these numbers is a square number?   _____

37–38 Which of these numbers are **prime numbers**?   _____ and _____

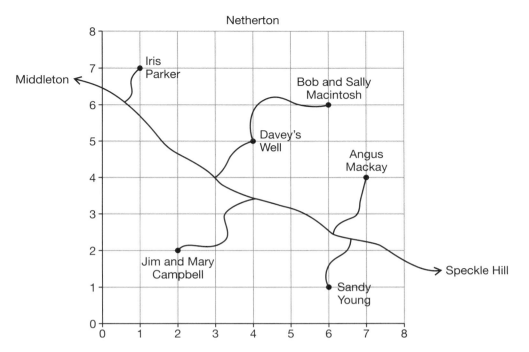

Netherton, on the Isle of Bacon, is a small hamlet with only a few houses. This map shows Netherton.

39–41 Who lives at these **coordinates**?

(1, 7) _____

(6, 1) _____

(6, 6) _____

42–43 What are the **coordinates** of these people's homes?

Angus Mackay (___ , ___)

Jim and Mary Campbell (___ , ___)

44 Which family has to pass the ancient Davey's Well to get to the main road?

_____

Badia is the apprentice at the local screws and nails factory. The other day she made some six-inch nails. Charli who works next to her made one and half times as many as Badia, but Siva made twice as many as Charli. They all made a total of 110 six-inch nails.

45 How many did Badia make? _____

46 How many did Charli make? _____

47 How many did Siva make? _____

49

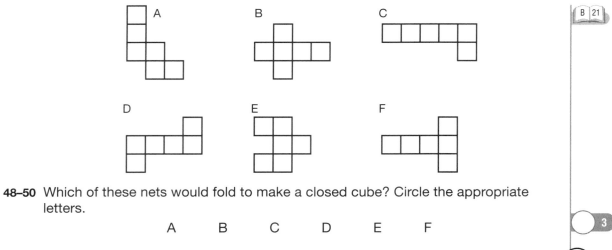

B 21

48–50 Which of these nets would fold to make a closed cube? Circle the appropriate
letters.

A   B   C   D   E   F

3

Now go to the Progress Chart to record your score!   Total   50

Paper 16

Find the three **prime factors** for each given number.

B5/B6

1–3 $30 = \underline{} \times \underline{} \times \underline{}$

4–6 $110 = \underline{} \times \underline{} \times \underline{}$

7–9 $165 = \underline{} \times \underline{} \times \underline{}$

9

B 20

x

x

$\frac{x}{2}$

$\frac{x}{2}$

$\frac{x}{2}$

$\frac{x}{2}$

10 What is the perimeter of this shape?

1

Underline the correct answer for each of these calculations.

11 $636 \div 12 =$ 5.3   50.3   35   53   530

12 $\frac{1}{7} + \frac{4}{21} =$ $\frac{7}{21}$ $\frac{5}{21}$ $\frac{5}{7}$ $\frac{5}{28}$ $\frac{7}{28}$

13 What % of 65 is 13?   30%   25%   20%   15%   10%

14 $2.05 - 0.15 =$ 1.009   9.01   9.1   1.09   1.9

Multiply these numbers by 100.

    15 0.27   _____

    16 0.035   _____

    17 0.101   _____

Divide these numbers by 1000.

    18 659   _____

    19 38   _____

    20 1.65   _____

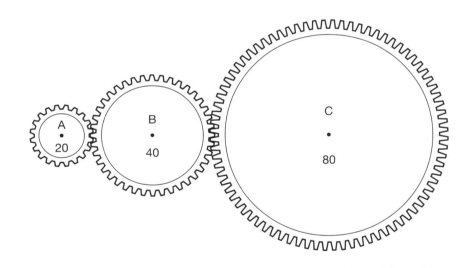

Here are three gear wheels. A has 20 teeth, B has 40 teeth, and C has 80 teeth.

If A makes 8 complete turns how many turns do the other gear wheels make?

    21 Gear B   _____

    22 Gear C   _____

If A made just one complete turn what fraction of a turn would each of the other gear wheels make?

    23 Gear B   _____

    24 Gear C   _____

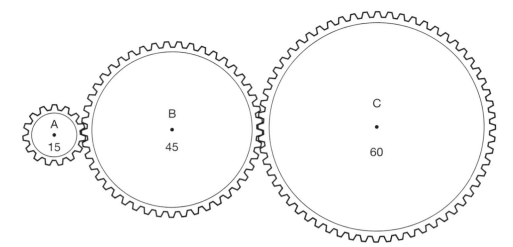

Here are three more gear wheels. In this arrangement A has 15 teeth, B has 45 teeth, and C has 60 teeth. If A makes four complete turns:

25 how many times does B rotate?   ___

26 how many times does C rotate?   ___

If B makes four complete turns:

27 how many times does A rotate?   ___

28 how many times does C rotate?   ___   **4**

These are the results of six children in three different tests:

Mathematics/30	English/50	Science/40
16	31	27
23	32	25
14	41	28
26	44	30
25	42	31
22	38	27

29 What is the **mean** Mathematics score?   ___

30 What is the **range** in Mathematics scores?   ___

31 What is the **mean** English score?   ___

32 What is the **range** in English scores?   ___

33 What is the **mean** Science score?   ___

34 What is the **range** in Science scores?   ___   **6**

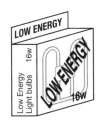
Pack of low
energy light bulbs
£4.29

Tin of paint
£7.99

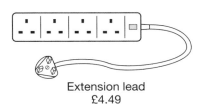
Extension lead
£4.49

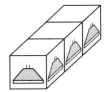
Pack of spotlights
£7.90

These are some of the prices at my DIY store. Use the prices to work out the answers to these money problems.

35 What change would I get from £20 if I bought 2 extension leads and 1 pack of spotlights?   £ _____

36 What change would I get from £40 if I bought 2 packs of low energy light bulbs and 3 tins of paint?   £ _____

37 What change would I get from £30 if I bought 1 pack of spotlights and 4 packs of low energy light bulbs?   £ _____

38 What change would I get from £25 if I bought one of each item?   _____ p

4

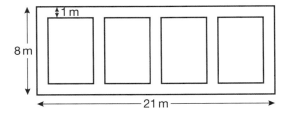

Here is a plan of Bill's allotment. He divides it into four equal sized plots and all of his paths are one metre wide. Use this information and what you can see on the plan to work out the answers to these questions.

39 What is the perimeter of the whole allotment?   ___ m

40 What is the area of each plot?   ___ m²

41 What is the perimeter of each plot?   ___ m

42 What is the area of the part of the path that goes around the edge of the allotment?   ___ m²

4

43–46 Put these values in order from largest to smallest.

$\frac{17}{50}$ 23% $\frac{2}{3}$ 78%   ___,   ___,   ___,   ___

4

47

48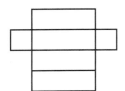

49

50

Using the terms tetrahedron, square-based pyramid, cuboid and open-topped cube, label each net above to show what 3-D shape it would make.

4

Now go to the Progress Chart to record your score! **Total** 50

Paper 17

Solve these calculations.

  1 $3.8 \times 6 =$ _____

  2 $9.24 \times 7 =$ _____

  3 $7.6 \times 8 =$ _____

  4 $8.51 \times 5 =$ _____

4

Solve these calculations.

  5 $289 \div 8.5 =$ _____

  6 $304 \div 1.6 =$ _____

  7 $89.6 \div 28 =$ _____

  8 $32.2 \div 1.4 =$ _____

4

Put the appropriate sign $<$, $>$ or $=$ in these calculations.

  9 (6×3.1) ___ $(10 + 9)$

  10 $(8 + 6.4)$ ___ (7.2×2)

  11 (3×3) ___ $(2 \times 2 \times 2)$

  12 $(4^2 - 3^2)$ ___ (3.5×2)

  13 (7.1×5) ___ 6^2

5

14–19 Here is a recipe for making apple flapjacks. Convert the imperial units to metric units. Remember that 1 ounce (oz) is approximately 25 grams (g) and 1 pound (lb) is 16 ounces (oz).

B 25

Apple Flapjacks	
IMPERIAL	METRIC
2 level tablespoons of golden syrup	2 level tablespoons of golden syrup
2 oz margarine	_____ g margarine
3 oz demerara sugar	_____ g demerara sugar
6 oz rolled oats	_____ g rolled oats
FILLING	
$1\frac{1}{5}$ oz margarine	_____ g margarine
1 lb cooking apples	_____ g cooking apples
$2\frac{2}{5}$ oz granulated sugar	_____ g granulated sugar

6

Work out what the letters x, y and z stand for in each of these equations.

B 8

20 $9x - 12 = 42$ $x =$ ____

21 $3y \div 2 = 12$ $y =$ ____

22 $6z + 30 = 48$ $z =$ ____

3

Now use the values that you have found for x, y and z to calculate the areas and perimeters of these rectangles.

B 20

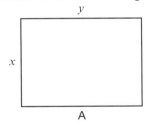
A

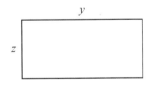
B   C

23–24 Rectangle A has an area of _____ cm² and a perimeter of _____ cm.

25–26 Rectangle B has an area of _____ cm² and a perimeter of _____ cm.

27–28 Rectangle C has an area of _____ cm² and a perimeter of _____ cm.

6

Find the answers to these calculations, writing your answer for each one in words.

B1/B2

29 $28 + 17 + 92 + 35 =$ _____

30 $109 + 151 + 106 + 204 =$ _____

31 $6.5 + 9.25 + 3.75 + 19.5 =$ _____

32 $30.6 + 28 + 70.4 + 56.5 =$ _____

_____

4

55

Dwayne collects stamps from four different countries. This table shows the number he has from each country.

USA	Canada	Australia	New Zealand
108	72	48	12

33 How many stamps does Dwayne have in total? _____

34 What fraction of these (in lowest terms) are from New Zealand? _____

35 What fraction of these (in lowest terms) are from the USA? _____

36 What percentage of these are from Australia? _____

37 What percentage of these are from Canada? _____

Round these figures to the nearest whole number.

38 21.6 _____

39 18.39 _____

40 1.71 _____

41 106.449 _____

42 60.81 _____

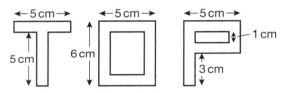

A sign-writer designed this stamp for boxes to show which way up they should be kept. All the letters are 1 cm wide.

43 What is the area of the letter T? _____

44 What is the area of the letter P? _____

45 What is the perimeter of the space in the centre of the letter O? _____

46 What is the perimeter of the outside of the letter P? _____

To design the stamp the sign-writer painted an example first. Every 3 cm² took one brush-load of paint.

47 How many times did he load up the brush to paint TOP? _____

At the local vegetable show Cruz, Seth and Joanna entered marrows in the largest marrow competition. Joanna's was $1\frac{1}{2}$ times as heavy as Seth's, and Cruz's was twice as heavy as Joanna's. The total weight of the three marrows was 33 lb.

48 What was the weight of Seth's marrow? _____ lb

49 What was the weight of Joanna's marrow? _____ lb

50 What was the weight of Cruz's marrow? _____ lb

Now go to the Progress Chart to record your score! **Total**

50

Paper 18

Fill in the missing numbers in these calculations.

B 3

1 23 × ___ = 276   **2** ___ × 21 = 315

3 18 × 11 = ___   **4** 37 × ___ = 148

5 ___ × 20 = 1920

5

Tariq kept a record of the number of hours he spent watching TV each week for 6 weeks. Here is what he recorded.

B 15

7   9   11   8   10   9

6 What is the **mean** number of hours?   ___

7 What is the **range**?   ___

2

Nini counted the number of skips she could do before she tripped. Here are her results for several tries.

B 15

35   38   34   33   37   37   31

8 What is the **mean** number of skips?   ___

9 What is the **range**?   ___

2

B 20

10 Chen-chi watched a snail take 2 hours to go round the edge of her patio. If the snail travelled 8 metres every hour, what is the perimeter of her patio?   _____

11 If her patio is square what is its area?   _____

2

B 21
B 22

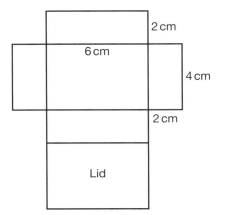

2 cm

6 cm

4 cm

2 cm

Lid

12 This diagram shows the net of a tin. What is the area of the lid?   _____ cm^2

13 What is the volume of the tin?   _____ cm^3

2

B 2

14 Three years ago Ravi had 2 collectable trains. Every year since he has bought 2 more trains. Calculate how many collectable trains Ravi will have in 2 years' time.   _____

1

London UK	Moscow Russia	San Francisco USA	Perth Australia	Rio de Janeiro Brazil
12:00	15:00	04:00	20:00	09:00

While it might be 12:00 in London, the digital clocks in other places show that the time there is different. Use the clocks shown here to answer these questions.

15 When it is 14:00 in London, what time will it be in Perth?   __ : __

16 When it is 16:30 in Rio de Janeiro, what time will it be in London?   __ : __

17 It is the same day in Moscow and San Francisco.
What is the difference in hours between the clocks?   __ hours

18 When it is 23:15 in Perth, what time will it be in Moscow?   __ : __

	OUT	**RETURN**
Great Summerfield	08:15	10:13
Little Summerfield	08:23	10:05
Edgeton	08:33	09:53
Leaside	08:41	09:44
Bridgeville	08:48	09:37
Malmington	08:56	09:30

This is part of the timetable for a local village bus service. Use it to answer these questions.

19 How much longer does it take to get from Malmington to
Great Summerfield than Great Summerfield to Malmington?   __ minutes

20 How long does it take to travel from Little Summerfield to Bridgeville?   __ minutes

21 How long does it take to travel from Little Summerfield to
Great Summerfield?   __ minutes

22 One morning the bus was delayed at Bridgeville for 12 minutes.
What time did it arrive at Edgeton?   __ : __

I received this parcel of books yesterday. After I had emptied it I opened it out flat for recycling.

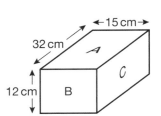

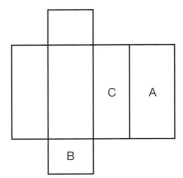

23 What is the perimeter of face A? _____ cm

24 What is the perimeter of face B? _____ cm

25 What is the perimeter of face C? _____ cm

26 What is the total area of the flattened box? _____ cm² ◯ 4

There are four strawberry crèmes to every three raspberry whirls in a box of chocolates. There are fifty-six chocolates altogether. 〔B 13〕

27–28 There are _____ strawberry crèmes and _____ raspberry whirls. ◯ 2

〔B 10〕

29–32 What proportion of the large rectangle (in **lowest terms**) is each of the smaller shapes?

A _____

B _____

C _____

D _____ ◯ 4

Solve these calculations. 〔B 3〕

33 304 ÷ 16 = _____

34 450 ÷ 18 = _____

35 896 ÷ 28 = _____

36 322 ÷ 14 = _____ ◯ 4

37–41 Debbie, who runs the village shop, went to the wholesalers to buy some things to sell in the shop. She adds 40% to the wholesale price to work out what the price in the shop will be. Complete this table. 〔B12/B2〕

	Wholesale price	**Profit (40%)**	**Shop price**
Item 1	£6.25	£2.50	£ _____
Item 2	£8.50	£ _____	£ _____
Item 3	£12.75	£ _____	£ _____

◯ 5

42–45 The exchange rate for Trinidad and Tobago dollars is 11.6 dollars ($) to the British pound (£). Complete this table.

B27/B2

British pounds (£)	Trinidad and Tobago dollars ($)
2	_____
5	_____
30	_____
75	_____

4

Determine the value of each of the letters in these equations.

46 $\dfrac{a}{25} = 60\%$ $a =$ ___

47 $\dfrac{b}{108} = \dfrac{3}{4}$ $b =$ ___

48 $4 \times c = 5$ $c =$ ___

49 $d + 6.5 = 17.25$ $d =$ ___

50 $\dfrac{(e + 3.5)}{40} = 20\%$ $e =$ ___

B 8
B10/B12
B 10
B 3
B2/B11
B10/B11
B 12

5

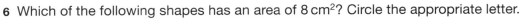

Now go to the Progress Chart to record your score!   **Total**   **50**

Paper 19

Fill in the missing numbers in these calculations.

B3/B2

1 $(8 \times$ ___ $) + 17 = 41$ **2** $28 = ($ ___ $\times 2) + 6$

3 $4 \times (66 -$ ___ $) = 36$ **4** $($ ___ $\div 9) - 6 = 6$

5 $(36 \div$ ___ $) + 80 = 92$

5

6 Which of the following shapes has an area of $8\,\text{cm}^2$? Circle the appropriate letter.

A a square with sides of $4\,\text{cm}$

B a triangle with a base of $2\,\text{cm}$ and a height of $2\,\text{cm}$

C a triangle with a base of $2\,\text{cm}$ and a height $4\,\text{cm}$

D a rectangle with sides of $2\,\text{cm}$ and $4\,\text{cm}$

B 18
B 20

1

7 The **mean** of the following 10 numbers is 2.4. Find the missing number.

2   6   1   2   3   ___   2   1   4   1

B 15

1

Put the correct sign $<$, $>$, $=$, $\div$, $\times$ in these calculations.

8 $405 \_\_\_ 27 = 15$

9 $(3.5 \times 3) \_\_\_ 7.5 + 2.75$

10 $(3 + 3 + 3 + 3 + 3) \_\_\_ (45 \div 3)$

Turn these fractions into percentages.

11 $\frac{17}{34} = \_\_\_ \%$

12 $\frac{9}{90} = \_\_\_ \%$

13 $\frac{28}{70} = \_\_\_ \%$

14 $\frac{36}{120} = \_\_\_ \%$

15 $\frac{55}{250} = \_\_\_ \%$

16–21 The Zap Electricity Company has added $7\frac{1}{2}\%$ surcharge to its bills. Complete this table for the surcharge and new bills for three of their customers.

	Bill	Surcharge	New bill
Mr Watt	£320	£ ____	£ ____
Ms Bright	£420	£ ____	£ ____
Mrs Brass	£472	£ ____	£ ____

Find the answers to these calculations.

22 $11.97 \,\text{km} - 2.75 \,\text{km} =$ _____ km

23 $3976 \,\text{cm} - 38.55 \,\text{m} =$ _____ m

24 $6 \times 406 \,\text{m} =$ _____ km

25 $5.78 \,\text{km} \div 34 =$ _____ m

A carpenter is making an outdoor game for his children. He draws a diagram showing where he should saw a sheet of plywood.

26 What is the area of part A? _____

27 What is the perimeter of part B? _____

28 What is the area of part C? _____

29 What is the perimeter of the whole sheet of plywood? _____

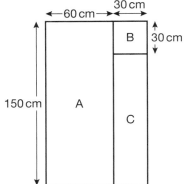

Turn these fractions into **mixed numbers** in their **lowest terms**.

30 $\frac{47}{20} =$ _____   **31** $\frac{125}{15} =$ _____   **32** $\frac{28}{3} =$ _____   **33** $\frac{174}{4} =$ _____

B 10

4

Turn these fractions into decimals.

34 $\frac{12}{25} =$ _____   **35** $\frac{6}{24} =$ _____   **36** $\frac{17}{85} =$ _____   **37** $\frac{6}{48} =$ _____

B10/B11

4

38–43 Insert the missing numbers to complete this multiplication table.

B 5

$\times$	__	__	__
__	6	12	14
__	12	24	28
__	24	48	56

6

B 17

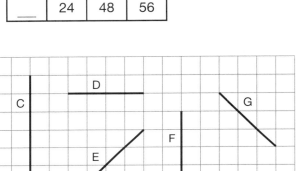

Circle TRUE or FALSE for each of these statements.

44 Line F is a vertical line.   TRUE   FALSE

45 Line G is perpendicular to D.   TRUE   FALSE

46 Line A is parallel to E.   TRUE   FALSE

47 Line B is perpendicular to C.   TRUE   FALSE

4

48–50 Fill in the missing numbers in this table.

B 15

Values					Mean of values
6	12	—	8	10	9
15	17	13	19	—	17
21	25	29	23	27	—

3

Paper 20

Find out the answers to these calculations.

1 $1.6 + 38.2 + 3.25 =$ _____ **2** $0.15 + 30.05 + 13.6 =$ _____

3 $31.6 + 0.45 + 10.32 =$ _____ **4** $20.05 + 21.75 + 1.69 =$ _____

5–8 Using the answers you have just found, order them from smallest to largest.

_____ _____ _____ _____

9 Melly was n years old last year. How old will she be in 4 years' time? _____ years

10 Here is a table showing the conversion of inches to centimetres.
Fill in the missing conversion.

Inches	Centimetres
7	17.78
8	_____
9	22.86
10	25.40

A car manufacturer has parked some new cars in two car parks. In the first car park there are 60 cars in the ratio 1 red car for every 2 blue cars and 3 silver cars. In the second car park there are 80 cars in the ratio 2 blue cars for every 3 red cars and 5 silver cars.

11 How many red cars are there altogether? _____

12 How many blue cars are there altogether? _____

13 How many silver cars are there altogether? _____

Calculate the values that the letters a, b, c, and d represent.

14 $a = 7^2 - 13$ $a =$ ___ **15** $b = (3.5 \times 12) \div 2$ $b =$ ___

16 $c = (45 - 9) \div 4$ $c =$ ___ **17** $d = (40\% \text{ of } 840) \div 8$ $d =$ ___

18–21 Now write the values that you have found in this table.

	Odd	Even
Square number	___	___
Not a square number	___	___

These were my scores at a local skittles evening.

33 37 39 41 34 38

22 What was my **mean** score? ___

23 What was the **range** of my scores? ___

63

B11/B2
8
B 8
1
B3/B25
1
B13/B2
3
B 8
B6/B2
B 11
B3/B12
8
B 15
2

24–29 Draw lines to connect the items on the left to their possible dimensions on the right.

B 25

Bucket of water	1 kg
Height of a man	200 km
Packet of sweets	5 litres
Distance from London to Birmingham	300 ml
Liquid in a bowl of soup	1 m 80 cm
Weight of a bag of sugar	100 g

6

640 people were asked which one of these BBC Radio stations they preferred to listen to. This pie chart shows the results:

B 14
B 12
B 2

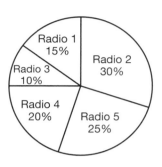

30 How many people prefer Radio 1? _____

31 How many people prefer Radio 4? _____

32 How many more people prefer Radio 2 than Radio 3? _____

33 Which radio station attracts as many listeners as Radio 1 and Radio 3 together? _____

4

34–39 Complete this table converting the digital clock times to a 12-hour clock time.

B 27

Digital time	12-hour clock time
06:30	_____
21:15	_____
01:12	_____
23:59	_____
14:06	_____
17:23	_____

6

Calculate the answers to these money problems, and then round your answer to the nearest pound.

B3/B1

40–41 £4.62 × 30 = £ _____ which is £ _____ to the nearest pound.

42–43 £9.76 × 40 = £ _____ which is £ _____ to the nearest pound.

44–45 £6.14 × 9 = £ _____ which is £ _____ to the nearest pound.

6

Divide these numbers by 1000.

B 1

46 496 _____   **47** 36 _____   **48** 11.1 _____

49 3.76 _____   **50** 0.52 _____

5

Now go to the Progress Chart to record your score!   Total   50

Paper 21

Find the answer to each of these problems.

1 In a leap year how many more days are there in May, June and July combined, than in January, February and March combined? _____

2 I enjoy making curry. The recipe that I like most uses two tablespoons of oil. There are 15 ml in a tablespoon. From a full bottle I can make 8 curries but I find that I have 10 ml of oil left over. How much oil is there in a full bottle? _____ ml

3 A local computer shop has a deal on a new computer that I would like to buy. They want a deposit of £115 and then 6 payments of £64. How much will the computer cost me? £ _____

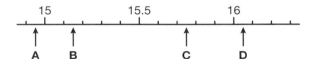

4–7 Which numbers are the arrows pointing to on this number line?

Arrow A _____   Arrow B _____   Arrow C _____   Arrow D _____

A local shop has these packs of paper for sale.

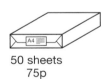

50 sheets
75p

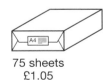

75 sheets
£1.05

100 sheets
£1.28

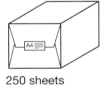

250 sheets
£3.25

8 If I want 150 sheets, what is the difference in price between buying one pack of 50 sheets plus one pack of 100 sheets, and buying two 75-sheet packs? _____ p

9 One day they had sold out of the 250-sheet packs. What is the difference in price between buying 2 packs of 75 sheets plus a 100-sheet pack, and buying 2 packs of 100 sheets plus a 50-sheet pack? _____ p

10 What is the difference between the cost of 6 packs of 50 sheets and 3 packs of 100 sheets? _____ p

Convert these **improper fractions** to **mixed numbers** in their **lowest terms**.

11 $\frac{57}{8}$ _____   **12** $\frac{34}{7}$ _____   **13** $\frac{46}{9}$ _____

In each row there is a number that can be divided exactly by each of the first pair or group of numbers given. Circle this number in each row.

14 3 and 8   12   16   24   30   36

15 6 and 12   18   24   30   42   50

16 2 and 5 and 7   40   50   60   70   80

17 3 and 6 and 5   12   18   30   36   49

18–23 Complete this table.

	Length	Width	Area	Perimeter
Rectangle 1	13 cm	6 cm	___ cm²	___ cm
Rectangle 2	___ cm	7 cm	84 cm²	___ cm
Rectangle 3	9 cm	___ cm	45 cm²	___ cm

24 Test tubes are sold in packs of four. A local technology college needs 282 test tubes. How many packs will they need to buy?   _____

There were 42 people who went on my class trip. Two sevenths of them were parents, and one seventh were teachers. The remainder were pupils.

25 How many parents were there?   _____

26 How many teachers were there?   _____

27 How many pupils were there?   _____

Work out the answers to these calculations.

28 $0.175 + 2.5 + 0.61 =$ _____

29 $1.09 + 1.63 + 0.44 =$ _____

30 $15.6 + 14.25 + 13.125 =$ _____

31 What are the **coordinates** of Mr Adam's farm?
(___ , ___)

32 What place lies west of Mr Adam's farm?

_____

33 What are its **coordinates**? (___ , ___)

34 What place is south-east of Mr Adam's farm?

_____

35 What are the **coordinates** of the building north of this place? (___ , ___)

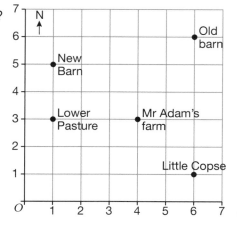

Here are some mathematics test results of nine children in Year 6. The test was out of 20.

B 15

16   18   14   18   12   16   11   18   12

36 What is the **range**? ___

37 What is the **mode**? ___

38 What is the **median**? ___

39 What is the **mean**? ___   4

Complete these sequences.

B7/B10

40 3.5   5   6.5   ___   9.5

41 $\frac{1}{2}$ $1\frac{3}{4}$ 3   ___ $5\frac{1}{2}$ 2

What is the value of number 6 in each of these figures?

B 1

42 1.65 ___   **43** 16.03 ___

44 162.54 ___   **45** 6023 ___   4

46–50 A local smallholder weighs all of his crops when he picks them. Here are the weights of five of the crops. Draw a bar chart to show these.

B 14

126 kilograms of beans,
108 kilograms of carrots,
95 kilograms of cabbages,
133 kilograms of potatoes,
64 kilograms of onions.

5

Paper 22

1–6 Round these numbers to complete the table. B 1

	To nearest 1000	To nearest 10 000	To nearest 100 000
163 712	_____	_____	_____
349 493	_____	_____	_____

6

Solve these calculations. B3/B11

7 $12 \times 14 =$ _____

8 $175 \div 3.5 =$ _____

9 $18 \times 2.5 =$ _____

10 $6.5 \times 9 =$ _____

4
B2/B3
B 25

Now solve these measures problems.

11 $683\,g + 836\,g =$ _____ kg

12 $23.6\,kg - 1540\,g =$ _____ kg

13 $6 \times 8.25\,kg =$ _____ kg

14 $5.79\,kg \div 6 =$ _____ g

4

15–18 Plot these **coordinates**: $(5, 2)$ $(-6, 2)$ $(3, -2)$ $(-4, -2)$ B23/B19

Connect the points to make a four-sided figure. B 24

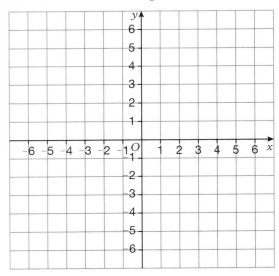

19 What is the shape called? _____

20 How many lines of symmetry does it have? _____

6

Find the answers to these calculations.

21 $(9 \times 3) - (9 \div 3) =$ ___

22 $(16 \times 4) - (16 \div 4) =$ ___

23 $(3 \times 16) \div 4 =$ ___

24 $\frac{3}{5}$ of $55 =$ ___

B2/B3
B8/B10
4

Pencil sharpener	Ruler	Pencil case	Coloured pencils	Geometry set	File
				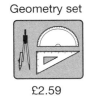	
99p	£1.19	£2.85	£4.75	£2.59	£2.59

B2/B3

Winston, Sarah, Sanjay and Emily went into the shop to buy some supplies for school.

25 Winston bought a ruler, a pencil case, and a file.
How much change did he get from £10? _____

26 Sarah bought a pencil sharpener, a pencil case, and some coloured
pencils. How much change did she get from £10? _____

27 Sanjay bought a pencil sharpener, a ruler, and a pencil case.
How much change did he get from £20? _____

28 Emily bought some coloured pencils, a geometry set, and a file.
How much change did she get from £20? _____

4
B2/B26
B 12

This bar chart shows the sorts of books in the class library.

29 How many books are there
altogether? ___

30 What % of the books are
storybooks? ___

31 What % of the books are reference
books? ___

32 What % of the books are nature
books? ___

33 What % of the books are science or
reference books? ___

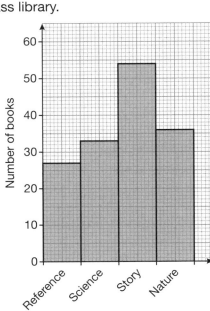

5

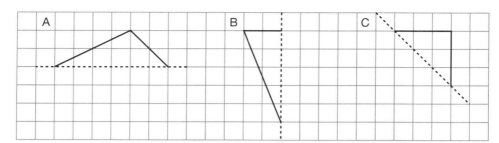

B24/B18
B 19

34–36 The dashed lines are mirror lines. Draw in the mirror images of these shapes.

What is the full name of each shape that you have made?

37 Shape A _____

38 Shape B _____

39 Shape C _____

6

40–45 Leo bought some sweets. He shared $\frac{4}{9}$ of each packet of sweets with his class. Complete this table to show how many sweets he shared and how many were left.

B10/B2

Sweet	Starting number	Sweets shared	Sweets remaining
Tom thumb drops	252	_____	_____
Micro mints	495	_____	_____
Tiny tots	369	_____	_____

6

B 17

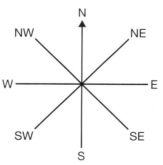

How many degrees do I turn if I move:

46 clockwise from NE to S? _____ °

47 clockwise from SE to N? _____ °

48 anti-clockwise from SW to NW? _____ °

What fraction of a complete turn (in **lowest terms**) do I make turning:

49 clockwise from E to SW? _____

50 anti-clockwise from W to N? _____

5

Paper 23

Calculate the answers.

B 10

1 $1003 - 8.7 =$ _____

2 $15 - 1.9 =$ _____

3 $795 - 9.1 =$ _____

4 $863 - 1.1 =$ _____

4

Solve these division problems.

B 3

5 $578 \div 34 =$ ___

6 $810 \div 45 =$ ___

7 $912 \div 16 =$ ___

8 $414 \div 23 =$ ___

4

9–14 A bookshop owner buys books from a wholesaler. She then adds 15% to the price paid before selling the books. Complete this table.

B12/B2

	Wholesale price	**15%**	**Shop price**
Book A	£6.80	_____	_____
Book B	£8.00	_____	_____
Book C	£10.60	_____	_____

6

15–20 Here is a timetable for a local bus service. Both buses take the same time to travel from one stop to the next. Enter the missing times for Bus B.

B2/B27

	Bus A	**Bus B**
Tetbury	11:17	14:52
Westonbirt	11:24	___ : ___
Willesley	11:26	___ : ___
Didmarton	11:29	___ : ___
Yate	11:46	___ : ___
Pucklechurch	12:00	___ : ___
Bath	12:35	___ : ___

6

What are these fractions as decimals?

B 11

21 $\frac{9}{10}$ _____

22 $\frac{7}{25}$ _____

23 $\frac{11}{20}$ _____

24 $\frac{3}{8}$ _____   **4**

What is the equivalent percentage for each of these fractions?

B 12

25 $\frac{49}{50}$ _____ %

26 $\frac{3}{50}$ _____ %

27 $\frac{21}{25}$ _____ %

28 $\frac{12}{75}$ _____ %   **4**

Circle the correct answer to each of these calculations.

B11/B3
B 10

29 $3.5 \times 300 =$ 950   1000   1050   1100

30 $70 \div 4 =$ 16 $16\frac{1}{2}$ 17 $17\frac{1}{2}$

31 $1003 - 13.9 =$ 989.1   998.1   898.1   889.1

32 $\frac{2}{3} + \frac{5}{6} =$ $1\frac{1}{6}$ $1\frac{1}{2}$ $1\frac{3}{4}$ $1\frac{2}{9}$

33 $0.5 \times 0.5 =$ 0.0025   0.025   0.25   2.5   **5**

B18/B20
B 2

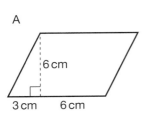

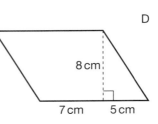

Calculate the areas of these **parallelograms**.

34 **Parallelogram** A has an area of _____ .

35 **Parallelogram** B has an area of _____ .

36 **Parallelogram** C has an area of _____ .

37 **Parallelogram** D has an area of _____ .   **4**

Calculate the answers to these multiplication problems.

38 $163 \times 12.6 =$ _____

39 $205 \times 2.5 =$ _____

40 $437 \times 0.7 =$ _____

41 $909 \times 1.9 =$ _____

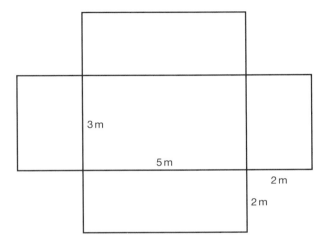

3 m

5 m

2 m

2 m

42 What is the volume of the fish tank that is represented by this net? _____

43 The **mean** of these numbers is 5. What is the value of a?

2   3   8   4 a 7   6

44 Sweet Tooth confectioners are going to mark their 50th anniversary by producing a limited edition chocolate bar. It will be 0.65 m long, 2 cm high and 1 cm deep.

What will be the volume of the chocolate bar? _____ m^3

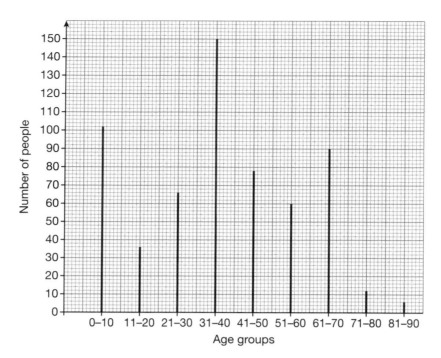

This is a bar-line chart showing the number of people, in different age groups, on a train trip.

What percentage of the passengers was in each of these age groups?

45 11–20 _____ %

46 31–40 _____ %

47 71–80 _____ %

48 What is the lowest percentage on the chart? _____ %

49 What is the percentage of the 51–60 and 61–70 age groups combined? _____ %

50 What is the difference in percentage between the youngest and the oldest age groups? _____ %

 6

Now go to the Progress Chart to record your score! **Total** 50

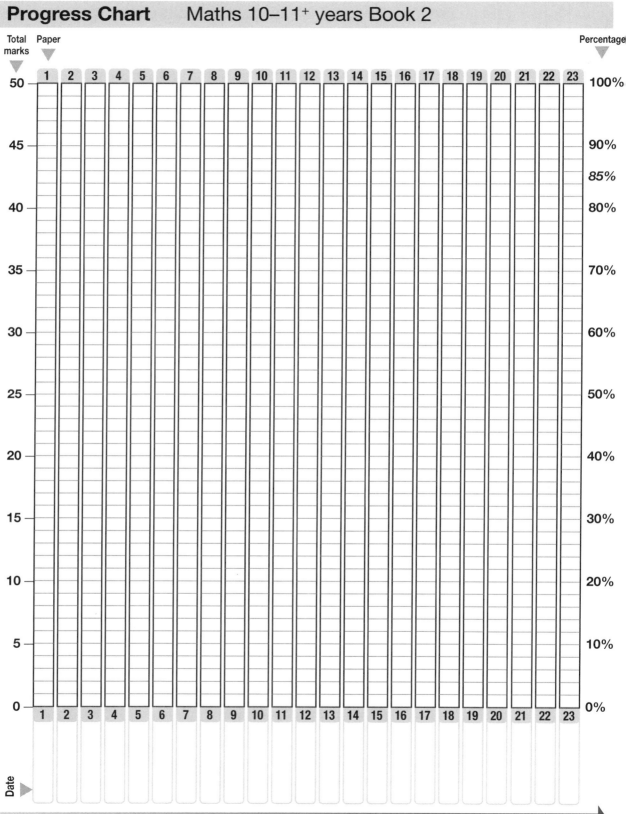

Progress Chart   Maths 10–11⁺ years Book 2

When you've finished the book use the Next Steps Planner